CHINESE TRADITIONAL CULTURE SERIES
中国传统文化精粹书系

Selected Poems and Pictures of the Song Dynasty

精选宋词与宋画
（英汉对照）

CHINA INTERCONTINENTAL PRESS
五洲传播出版社

Contents

目录

Preface

After the mid-10th century, a new unified dynasty called Song (960-1279) was established in China, which replaced the 54-year-old Five Dynasties (907-960) during which the nation was carved up into a number of separate regimes by rival warlords. At the beginning of the Song Dynasty, a rehabilitation policy was adopted, aiming to diminish the social repercussion caused by the dynastic change and help restore agriculture and handicraft to the original level as seen in the Tang Dynasty (618-907). Eventually, the Song saw an agricultural growth exceeding that of all the previous dynasties in history.

The urban business economy was thriving accordingly. *The Festival of Pure Brightness on the River* by Zhang Zeduan delineates the metropolitan life on both sides of the Bianhe River in the Northern Song (960-1127) capital Kaifeng during the Qingming (Pure Brightness) Festival. Economic prosperity and population growth also helped turn south China into a developed region. Thus the Yangtze River basin became another economic and cultural center of the country following the Yellow River.

A prosperous society made it possible for the development of literature and art. *Ci* poetry, originating in the Tang and written to certain tunes in fixed numbers of lines and words, was fully developed in the Song. Composing *ci* poems became a common and fashionable practice among the literati. The school of *haofang* (heroic abandon)

represented by Su Shi (or Su Shih, 1037-1101) and Xin Qiji (or Hsin Ch'i-chi, 1140-1207) and that of *wanyue* (restraint and subtlety) by Li Qingzhao (1084-c.1151) and Liu Yong (c.971-1053) were the most well known then. *Ci* poetry is quite particular about meter and rhyme scheme. Most *ci* poems are of profound implications. Along with Tang poetry, *ci* is a treasure house of China's ancient literature, read with admiration by people over hundreds of years.

The Song government set up a huge imperial art academy to enlist talented and pioneering painters, who scored considerable achievements in figure, genre, history, landscape and flower-and-bird paintings, and left behind a great amount of enduring works. Those noted artists included: figure painter Li Gonglin; genre painters Zhang Zeduan, Su Hanchen and Li Song; landscape painters Dong Yuan, Ju-ran, Li Cheng, Fan Kuan, Guo Xi, Mi Fu, Mi Youren, Li Tang, Liu Songnian, Ma Yuan, Xia Gui, Zhao Baiju and Zhao Bosu; flower-and-bird painters Zhao Ji (Emperor Huizong), Huang Jucai, Zhao Chang, Yi Yuanji, Li Di, Lin Chun and Fa-chang.

Song painters came to see the art of painting in a new light. Poet and painter Su Shi not only left behind imperishable artworks in large quantities, but also advanced the theory of "There is painting in poetry just as there is poetry in painting." This has become an artistic conception sought by painters of later ages.

In this book are contained some selected Song Dynasty *ci* poems and paintings, with English interpretations, so that readers of different language and cultural background can enjoy their beauty together.

序

宋朝（960-1279）时，中国在世界上是首屈一指的国家。10世纪中后叶，宋代结束了中国自唐代（618-907）以后五代（907-960）时期50多年的分而治之的割据局面。宋初，政府采取政策，促进社会发展，使经济恢复到唐代原有的水平。城市的商业经济在宋代开始兴旺起来，宋代画家张择端所绘的著名的《清明上河图》描绘的就是北宋（960-1127）都城汴梁（今开封）一带繁荣的社会生活景象。经济机会和人口增加使南方大部分地区发达起来，长江流域像黄河流域一样，成为中国的经济文化中心。

宋代的社会繁荣，为其文学艺术的发展提供了广阔的空间和有利条件。宋词成为和唐诗相提并论的中国古代文学的另一座高峰。宋代人填词成为时尚，"文人学子相聚，凡不能一道背诵其诗词者，皆自惭形秽。"宋代大词人以苏轼、辛弃疾为代表的豪放派和以李清照、柳永为代表的婉约派最为著名。宋词韵律优美，意境幽远，意味深长，具有独特的魅力，甚至有人认为吟诵宋词或许可以使人灵秀。

宋代立国后，便设置了"翰林图画院"，网罗各地的画家。宋代画家视野扩大，并对各种题材进行了分门别类的研究，反映现实生活的人物画、风俗画，描写历史的历史画，描绘壮丽河山的山水画以及富丽锦簇的花鸟画都有开拓性和长足的发展，留下了大量的传世佳作。著名的画家更是不计其数，如擅长人物画的李公麟，风俗画的张择端、苏汉臣、李嵩，山水画的董源、巨然、李成、范宽、郭熙、米芾、米友仁、李唐、刘松年、马远、夏圭、赵佰驹、赵伯骕等，花鸟画的宋徽宗赵佶、黄居寀、赵昌、易元吉、李迪、林椿、法常等。

宋代的画家对绘画艺术有了进一步的理解。宋代大文学家、画家苏轼（1037-1101）不仅留下了大量不朽的词作和画作，而且提出了"诗中有画，画中有诗"的主张，成为后来历代画家追求的境界。

本书精选部分宋词和宋画，并配以英文翻译，以期和更多不同语言文化背景的读者共享宋词与宋画之美。

TUNE: ROUGED LIPS
REFLECTION
— Wang Yucheng

Laden with frowning cloud and steeped in tearful rain, the southern shores still beautiful remain. In riverside village flanked with fishermen's fair, a lonely wreath of slender smoke wafts in the air.

Afar a row of wild geese fly, weaving a letter in the sky. What have I done in days gone by? Gazing from the balustrade, could I weave my way as far as they?

注 释

①"天际征鸿"句：天际行鸿雁，遥远地看去它们远征的轨迹如一线连缀。

②凝睇：凝眸

diǎn jiàng chún
点 绛 唇
gǎn xìng
感 兴
wāng yǔ chěng
—— 王禹偁

yǔ hèn yún chóu　　jiāng nán yī jiù chēng jiā
雨 恨 云 愁 ， 江 南 依 旧 称 佳

lì　　shuǐ cūn yú shì　　yì lǚ gū yān xì
丽 。 水 村 渔 市 ， 一 缕 孤 烟 细 。

tiān jì zhēng hóng　　yáo rèn háng rú zhuì①
天 际 征 鸿 ， 遥 认 行 如 缀①。

píng shēng shì　　cǐ shí níng dì②　　shuí huì píng
平 生 事 ， 此 时 凝 睇②， 谁 会 凭

lán yì
栏 意 ？

Seeking the Tao in Autumn Mountains by Ju-ran, Northern Song, hanging scroll, ink on silk, 156.2 x 77.2 cm, kept in the Palace Museum of Taipei. Ju-ran was originally a brush painter of the Southern Tang (937-975). Taking Dong Yuan as a model, his early paintings were simple but full of childish playfulness. After submitting to the authority of the Northern Song, influenced by the northern school, he added landscape depiction to his drawings as seen in this picture, one of his representative works. Ju-ran further developed Dong's method of showing the shades and texture of rocks and mountains by light ink strokes. Therefore he was regarded as an important painter in the evolution of the ancient mountains-and-waters painting.

◎ 秋山问道图轴，北宋，巨然，绢本墨笔，156.2×77.2cm，台北故宫博物院藏。巨然原为南唐（937-975）画家，归宋后，画风受到北方画派的一定影响，与以前师法董源时追求的平淡天真有所不同，在创作中增添了高山大川的描绘，《秋山问道图》便是此时的代表作品。此图在追求上虽有所变化，但对老师董源所创的"披麻皴"作了进一步的发展，从而使巨然成为文人山水画发展进程中的一位重要画家。

TUNE: TREADING ON GRASS

— Kou Zhun

Springtime is on the wane; the oriole's song grows old, all red flowers fallen and green mume fruit still small. Quiet is painted hall despite the drizzling rain, half-hidden by the screen a wreath of incense cold.

Our vow deep, deep in the heart, we're sad to be far, far apart. I will not look into my brass mirror dust-grey. Silent, I lean on rails, my soul pining away; my longing like green grass would join the vast dim sky, alas!

踏莎行

—— 寇准

春色将阑①，莺声渐老，
红英落尽青梅小②。画堂人静
雨蒙蒙，屏山半掩余香袅。
密约沉沉，离情杳杳，菱
花尘满慵将照③。倚楼无语欲
销魂，长空黯淡连芳草。

注释

①阑：将近。此处指春天已尽尾声。
②红英：红色的花瓣。英，花。
③"菱花"句：菱花，指镜子。慵，慵懒。这句是说菱花镜上落满了灰尘，主人慵懒地将它拿起，准备照一照自己的容颜。

6

Hibiscus and Golden Pheasant by Zhao Ji (Emperor Huizong), Northern Song, hanging scroll, color on silk, 81.5 x 53.6 cm, kept in the Palace Museum of Beijing. The painter used vivid touches to portray a golden pheasant in the foreground, two butterflies fluttering on the top right corner and swaying blossoming branches on the backdrop. A careful depiction of the bird's colorful feathers demonstrates the artist's superb realistic skill.

◎ 芙蓉锦鸡图轴，北宋，赵佶即宋徽宗（1100—1126年在位），绢本设色，81.5×53.6cm，北京故宫博物院藏。此图设色花芙蓉、菊花，双钩工整。锦鸡回首，仰望双蝶戏飞。这幅画写实技巧相当高超，锦鸡羽毛的华美细致斑纹、芙蓉花枝因锦鸡停栖其上的摇曳动荡之姿，都刻画得传神逼真。

TUNE: FOUNTAIN OF WINE

— Pan Lang

I still remember West Lake, where, leaning on the rails, I gazed without a break on fishing boats in twos and threes and islets in clear autumn breeze.

Among flowering reeds faint flute-songs rose, startled white birds took flight in rows. Since I left, I've repaired my fishing rod at leisure, thoughts of waves and clouds thrill me with pleasure.

酒泉子
jiǔ quán zǐ

——潘阆
pān làng

长 忆 西 湖 ， 尽 日 凭 栏 楼
cháng yì xī hú，jìn rì píng lán lóu
上 望 。 三 三 两 两 钓 鱼 舟 ， 岛
shàng wàng。sān sān liǎng liǎng diào yú zhōu，dǎo
屿 正 清 秋 ① 。
yǔ zhèng qīng qiū

笛 声 依 约 芦 花 里 ， 白 鸟
dí shēng yī yuē lú huā lǐ，bái niǎo
成 行 忽 惊 起 。 别 来 闲 整 钓 鱼
chéng háng hū jīng qǐ。bié lái xián zhěng diào yú
竿 ， 思 入 水 云 寒 ② 。
gān，sī rù shuǐ yún hán

注 释

① 岛屿：此处指西湖上的小岛。
② "思入水云寒"句：在闲闲地整理钓鱼竿的同时，思绪不自觉地飘飞到了水天相接，云生雾绕的远方。

Crane by Fa-chang, Southern Song, hanging scroll, ink and wash on silk, 173.9 x 98.8 cm, kept in Daitokuji Temple in Kyoto, Japan. It's the left one of a trio of hanging scrolls; the other two are *Guanyin* (C) and *Monkeys* (R). In the painting a crane is strolling out of a bamboo forest enveloped in mist and clouds. The crane was drawn with fine, exquisite strokes, combining both delicate and freehand brushwork. The bamboos were painted in ink and wash with a novel technique that was rarely tried by previous painters.

◎ 鹤图，法常，立轴，绢本水墨，173.9×98.8cm，日本京都大德寺藏。法常所作的此图原是和《观音图》《猿图》合为一套三联立轴，其为左轴画。图中一只仙鹤，昂首清啼，步出竹林。周围云蒸雾绕，仙韵十足。笔法轻俊有致，墨色酣畅多变。鹤的用笔较细致，工写兼备。以水墨画竹林，墨色浓淡变化自如，这在前人是颇为少见的。

TUNE: EVERLASTING LONGING

— Lin Bu

Northern hills green, southern hills green, the green hills greet your ship sailing between. Who knows my parting sorrow keen?

Tears from your eyes, tears from mine eyes, could silken girdle strengthen our heart-to-heart ties? O see the river rise!

cháng xiāng sī
长 相 思

—— lín bū
—— 林 逋

wú shān qīng yuè shān qīng liǎng
吴 山 青①， 越 山 青②， 两

àn qīng shān xiāng sòng yíng shuí zhī lí bié
岸 青 山 相 送 迎 ， 谁 知 离 别

qíng
情 ？

jūn lèi yíng qiè lèi yíng luó dài
君 泪 盈 ， 妾 泪 盈③， 罗 带

tóng xīn jié wèi chéng jiāng tóu cháo yǐ píng
同 心 结 未 成④， 江 头 潮 已 平 。

注 释

①吴：指今江苏一带地方。

②越：指今浙江一带地方。

③妾：古时女子谦称自己。

④罗带：丝制的绸带。古代男女定情时，往往将其打成一个心形的结，叫做"同心结"。此句中"结未成"，暗喻了他们爱情的不幸。

Almond Blossoms by Zhao Chang, Northern Song, round fan, color on silk, 25.2 x 27.3 cm, kept in the Palace Museum of Taipei. The painter portrays with realistic technique an almond tree in full blossom.

◎ 杏花图，赵昌，团扇，绢本设色，25.2 × 27.3cm，中国台北故宫博物院藏。此图绘一只杏花，繁花盛开。画家用极写实的手法，将杏花粉白含俏、堆霜集雪之姿，刻画得栩栩如生，勾线精细，以粉白染瓣，富有层次。杏花尽显晶莹剔透、冰姿雪清之雅韵。

TUNE: JOY OF DAY AND NIGHT

—Liu Yong

In nuptial bed for the first time we met, I thought forever we'd together get. The short-lived joy of love, who would believe? Soon turned to parting that would grieve. When late spring has grown old and soon takes leave, I see a riot of catkins and flowers fallen in showers. I am afraid all the fine view would go with you.

To whom may I complain of my solitude? You oft make light of promise you have made. Had I known the ennui is so hard to elude, I would then have you stayed. What I can't bear to think, your gallantry apart, is something else in you captivating my heart. If one day I don't think of it, a thousand times it would make my brows knit.

Turtledove on Peach by Zhao Ji (Emperor Huizong), Northern Song, album leaf, color on silk, 26.4 x 28.5 cm, kept in the National Museum of Tokyo, Japan. Despite its simple composition, this picture drawn with rich color presents a refined and stately appearance. It's said that the painting was made by Zhao at age 26.

◎ 桃鸠图，宋徽宗赵佶，册页，绢本设色，26.4 × 28.5cm，日本东京国立博物馆藏。在相传是宋徽宗的作品中，这件册页比较特别，仅绘有一枝桃花一只鸟，但仍能显现出富贵与典雅的气象。图中桃花与桃叶勾勒工精，桃枝染色浓重而伸展遒劲，栖鸠动态自然而生动，用生漆点睛，卓有神采，整体色彩华丽。据传这是宋徽宗 26 岁时的作品。

昼夜乐

——柳永

洞房记得初相遇，便只合长相聚。何期小会幽欢，化作别离情绪？况值阑珊春色暮①，对满目乱花狂絮，直恐好风光，尽随伊归去②。

一场寂寞凭谁诉？算前言总轻负③。早知恁的难拚④，悔不当初留住。其奈风流端正外⑤，更别有系人心处。一日不思量，也攒眉千度⑥。

注　释

①阑珊：将尽。此地指春又归去。

②伊：他。在柳永的俗词中，"伊"一般用以指男性。

③轻负：以前说的话不作数，辜负了对方。

④恁的：这么样，如此。

⑤其奈：怎奈。

⑥攒眉：皱眉，愁眉紧锁的样子。

Hollyhock, author unknown, Southern Song (1127-1279), round fan, color on silk, 25.4 x 25.9 cm, kept in Shanghai Museum. After losing the territory of north China, the Southern Song regime was content to retain control over south China. Public morals were deteriorating day by day. Under such circumstances, the imperial-court decorative painting tended to be miniaturized, focusing on single flower or bird. Citing this picture, despite its excessively delicate depiction, it seems to appeal to decadent tastes.

◎ 蜀葵图，南宋（1127-1279），佚名，团扇，绢本设色，25.4 × 25.9cm，上海博物馆藏。宋王朝疆土至南宋时已经大为缩小，更加上统治者偏安一隅，沉迷于生活的小情趣中，影响所及，宫体绘画中的花鸟也多为单枝独柯。以此图为例，尽管画面描绘细致工整，花开之姿分外妖娆，但在丰润秀丽、卓有生气之外，也不免使人有柔靡之叹。

TUNE: BELLS RINGING IN THE RAIN

— Liu Yong

Cicadas chill drearily shrill. We stand face to face in an evening hour before the pavilion, after a sudden shower. Can we care for drinking before we part? At the city gate we are lingering late, but the boat is waiting for me to depart. Hand in hand we gaze at each other's tearful eyes and burst into sobs with words congealed on our lips. I'll go my way far, far away on miles and miles of misty waves where sail ships, and evening clouds hang low in boundless Southern skies.

Lovers would grieve at parting as of old. How could I stand this clear autumn day so cold! Where shall I be found at daybreak from wine awake? Moored by a riverbank planted with willow trees beneath the waning moon and in the morning breeze. I'll be gone for a year. In vain would good times and fine scenes appear. However gallant I am on my part, to whom can I lay bare my heart?

Flower Basket by Li Song, Southern Song, album leaf, color on silk, 19.1 x 26.5 cm, kept in the Palace Museum of Beijing. Li, a court painter serving under three emperors in succession, was well versed in figure, landscape and flower-and-bird painting. This still-life drawing fully reflects the attainments achieved by Song Dynasty flower-and-bird painters.

◎ 花篮图页，南宋，李嵩，绢本设色，19.1 × 26.5cm，北京故宫博物院藏。李嵩是南宋历经三朝的画院待诏，工画人物、山水、花鸟，强调摹写自然。此图描绘在精美的花篮中盛开的鲜花，用色凝重艳丽，用笔谨严有序，充分反映了宋代工笔花鸟所达到的写实高度。

雨霖铃

——柳永

寒蝉凄切①，对长亭晚，骤雨初歇。都门帐饮无绪②，方留恋处，兰舟催发③。执手相看泪眼，竟无语凝噎④。念去去千里烟波，暮霭沉沉楚天阔⑤。

多情自古伤离别，更哪堪冷落清秋节！今宵酒醒何处？杨柳岸晓风残月。此去经年，应是良辰好景虚设。便纵有千种风情⑥，更与何人说！

注 释

①寒蝉：即寒螀，似蝉而小，亦名蜩，入秋始鸣。凄切：凄惨而又急促的声响。

②都门帐饮：都门，指京城，这里指汴京（今河南开封市）。帐饮：在郊外张设帷帐，摆宴送别。

③方留恋处：《彊村丛书》本作"留恋处"，于律应为四字句。此据《汲古阁本》。兰舟：木兰之舟，喻船之华美。

④凝噎：声凝语噎，悲泣之状。

⑤暮霭：暮色，傍晚的云气。楚天：这里指运河下游，江淮一带。

⑥风情：柔情。

Pheasant and Small Birds by a Jujube Shrub by Huang Jucai, Northern Song, hanging scroll, color on silk, 99 x 53.6 cm, kept in the Palace Museum of Taipei. It shows a well-balanced composition. With a delicately painted pheasant in the foreground and lovely birds chirping on the twigs of a jujube shrub, the picture was drawn in a vivid and lively style.

◎山鹧棘雀图轴，北宋，黄居寀，绢本设色，99×53.6cm，台北故宫博物院藏。此图画野水坡石，竹草棘枝衬出神采各异的鸟雀。画中鹧、雀或谛听，或顾盼，或飞鸣，或栖止，种种瞬间的动作都被表现得真实生动。又着意刻画近处的山鹧，红嘴黑头，白羽飘逸。布景匀称，意境平和，笔法稳健，形象逼真。

TUNE: PHOENIX PERCHING ON PLANE TREE

— Liu Yong

I lean alone on balcony in light, light breeze; as far as the eye sees, on the horizon dark parting grief grows unseen. In fading sunlight rises smoke over grass green. Who understands why mutely on the rails I lean?

I'd drown in wine my parting grief; chanting before the cup, strained mirth brings no relief. I find my gown too large, but I will not regret; it's worth while growing languid for my coquette.

凤 栖 梧
fèng qī wú

—— 柳 永
liǔ yǒng

伫倚危楼风细细①，望极
zhù yǐ wēi lóu fēng xì xì wàng jí
春愁，黯黯生天际。草色烟光
chūn chóu àn àn shēng tiān jì cǎo sè yān guāng
残照里，无言谁会凭栏意？
cán zhào lǐ wú yán shuí huì píng lán yì
拟把疏狂图一醉，对酒当
nǐ bǎ shū kuáng tú yī zuì duì jiǔ dāng
歌，强乐还无味。衣带渐宽终
gē qiǎng lè huán wú wèi yī dài jiàn kuān zhōng
不悔，为伊消得人憔悴②。
bù huǐ wèi yī xiāo dé rén qiáo cuì

注 释

①伫倚危楼：伫立在那里依偎着高楼。

②"衣带"二句：衣带渐渐显出宽松最终也不后悔，为了她竟使人变得消瘦而憔悴。此句后被王国维喻为治学的第二大境界。

Reed Pond Under Thick Snow by Liang Shimin, Northern Song, handscroll, color on silk, 26.5 x 145.8 cm, kept in the Palace Museum of Beijing. Liang was Emperor Huizong's court painter, and this scroll is his only work left behind. A pair of wild ducks swims in a snow-covered reed pond in the dusk of the evening. The composition was precisely and delicately arranged.

◎ 芦汀密雪图卷，北宋，梁师闵，绢本设色，26.5×145.8cm，北京故宫博物院藏。梁师闵是宋徽宗时的朝廷官员，工于诗画，深得皇帝青睐。他的传世作品仅此一图。从画面的款识来看，这件作品似乎是专为御览而作。图中描绘了暮雪芦塘，有野兔一对，鸳鸯一双，画面精致而不疏放，笔墨也十分谨严，显示了画家在创作给皇帝看的作品时特有的小心谨慎态度。

TUNE: PRIDE OF FISHERMEN

— Fan Zhongyan

When autumn comes to the frontier, the scene looks drear; southbound wild geese won't stay e'en for a day. An uproar rises with horns blowing far and near. Walled in by peaks, smoke rises straight at sunset over isolate town with closed gate.

I hold a cup of wine, yet home is far away; the northwest not yet won, I can't but stay. At the flutes' doleful sound over frost-covered ground, none falls asleep; the general's hair turns white and soldiers weep.

注　释

①塞下：边塞一带。

②衡阳雁去：即"雁去衡阳"之倒装。湖南衡阳有回雁峰。相传北雁南飞至此即止。

③边声：泛指边境上的各种令人心惊的声响，如风号、马鸣、悲笳、鼓角之类。

④千嶂：形容群山环绕，有如屏障。

⑤"燕然"句：指敌人未灭，不能回家。燕然：山名，即今蒙古人民共和国的杭爱山。后汉窦宪追击北匈奴至此，刻石纪功而还。勒：刻。

⑥羌管：即羌笛，出自羌族，故名。

渔家傲

—— 范仲淹

塞下秋来风景异①，衡阳雁去无留意②，四面边声连角起③。千嶂里④，长烟落日孤城闭。

浊酒一杯家万里，燕然未勒归无计⑤。羌管悠悠霜满地⑥。人不寐，将军白发征夫泪。

山禽矜逸態
梅粉弄輕柔
已有丹青約
千秋指白頭

Wild Birds on Wild Prunus by Zhao Ji (Emperor Huizong), Northern Song, color on silk, 82.8 x 52.8cm, kept in the Palace Museum of Taipei. Huizong, well known as a literati emperor devoted to prose and poetry, was skilled in calligraphy and painting. He was talented in figure, landscape and bird-and-flower paintings. He fully demonstrated his preeminent talent for poetry, calligraphy and painting in this work, on which he inscribed a pentasyllabic verse in the *shou-chin* ("slender gold") style.

◎ 腊梅山禽图轴，宋徽宗赵佶，绢本设色，82.8 × 52.8cm，台北故宫博物院藏。宋徽宗秉赋极高，笔砚、丹青、图史、射御皆精。爱好书画，人物、山水、花鸟均见长，笔墨挺秀，别具一格。这幅画用瘦金书自题五绝一首，显示出徽宗诗书画三绝之才华。

TUNE: SONG OF WATER CLOCK

— Zhang Xian

The banquet spread in red with silken screen in green, attended by maidens fair of fifteen or sixteen, alone she knows to care for talents fine and fill my cup with wine.

With long brows green and small mouth, she would lean on me and whisper in my ear: "The winding willowy way is near the house where you'll find me. In front there is a blossoming apricot tree."

gēng lòu zǐ
更 漏 子

zhāng xiān
—— 张 先

jǐn yán hóng　　luó mù cuì　　shì yàn měi
锦 筵 红 ， 罗 幕 翠 ， 侍 宴 美

rén shū lì①　　shí wǔ liù　　jiě lián cái②
人 姝 丽① 。 十 五 六 ， 解 怜 才② ，

quàn rén shēn jiǔ bēi
劝 人 深 酒 杯 。

dài méi cháng　　tán kǒu xiǎo③　　ěr pàn
黛 眉 长 ， 檀 口 小③ ， 耳 畔

xiàng rén qīng dào　　liǔ yīn qū　　shì ér
向 人 轻 道 ： " 柳 阴 曲 ， 是 儿

jiā　　mén qián hóng xìng huā
家 ， 门 前 红 杏 花 。 "

注 释

①姝丽：美好娇丽。

②解怜才：懂得怜惜有才之士。

③檀口：古时女子以檀香作化妆品，嘴角抹檀香因此将其口称做檀口。

One Hundred Children at Play (partial) by Su Hanchen, Southern Song, handscroll, color on silk, 30.6 x 525.5 cm, kept in the Palace Museum of Taipei. In the painting a kid is watching goldfish, two are wrestling with each other, and some others are playing. A figure painter, Su was especially good at portraying children's life.

◎ 长春百子（局部），南宋，苏汉臣，绢本设色，30.6 × 525.5cm（卷），台北故宫博物院藏。苏汉臣专长人物画，尤善描写儿童生活。画面描写了几个儿童玩耍嬉戏的场面。有的在观金鱼，有的在摔跤，宋代儿童生活情趣跃然纸上。

TUNE: SONG OF THE IMMORTAL

—Zhang Xian

Wine cup in hand, I listen to Water Melody,
awake from wine at noon, but not from melancholy.
When will spring come back now it is going away?
In the mirror, alas! I see happy time pass. In vain
may I recall the old days gone for aye.

Night falls on poolside sand where pairs of love-
birds stay; the moon breaks through the clouds, with
shadows flowers play. Lamplights veiled by screen
on screen can't be seen. The fickle wind still blows;
the night so silent grows. Tomorrow fallen reds
should cover the pathway.

天仙子

tiān xiān zǐ

—— 张 先
zhāng xiān

水 调 数 声 持 酒 听①, 午 醉
shuǐ diào shù shēng chí jiǔ tīng   wǔ zuì

醒 来 愁 未 醒 。 送 春 春 去 几 时
xǐng lái chóu wèi xǐng   sòng chūn chūn qù jǐ shí

回 ? 临 晚 镜 , 伤 流 景 , 往 事 后
huí   lín wǎn jìng   shāng liú jǐng   wǎng shì hòu

期 空 记 省②。
qī kōng jì xǐng

沙 上 并 禽 池 上 暝③, 云
shā shàng bìng qín chí shàng míng   yún

破 月 来 花 弄 影④。 重 重 帘 幕
pò yuè lái huā nòng yǐng   chóng chóng lián mù

密 遮 灯⑤。 风 不 定 , 人 初 静 ,
mì zhē dēng   fēng bù dìng   rén chū jìng

明 日 落 红 应 满 径 。
míng rì luò hóng yīng mǎn jìng

注 释

①"水调"句:把盏听唱《水调》。
《水调》是词牌名,作为隋炀帝开
运河所用。
②"往事"句:夜间对镜,想起伤
心过往,记忆中的一切也是徒自
令人感伤。记省,清楚记得。
③"沙上"句:沙洲上成双的水鸟
在池塘边歇息。暝,闭眼小憩。
④"云破"句:风吹云散,月光乍
现,花也在风中摇晃弄影。
⑤"重重"句:室内重重帘幕密密
地遮住来风,护住灯烛不为吹灭。

Pavilions and Mansions by Rivers and Mountains by Yan Wengui, Northern Song, hanging scroll, ink and wash on silk, 103.9 x 47.4 cm, kept in the Palace Museum of Taipei. During the Northern Song Dynasty, many painters first acquired a reputation in the public eye, and then were admitted to the imperial art academy. Yan was among them. Initially he made a living by selling paintings in Kaifeng, the Northern Song capital. After coming to fame, he was taken to the palace and became a court painter for Emperor Zhenzong. This scroll is one of his enduring works, expressing the grandeur of nature using only ink and touches of color.

◎ 溪山楼观图轴，北宋，燕文贵，绢本水墨，103.9 × 47.4cm，台北故宫博物院藏。北宋的职业画家十分活跃，有许多技艺卓绝的画家就是首先在社会上获得广泛的声名以后，引起皇室注意，才被召入宫廷画院。燕文贵就是这样的画家。最初时，燕文贵在汴梁州桥卖画，声名鹊起而入宫廷，成为宋真宗时画院画师。这件作品为其传世之作，画面构图突兀，气象不凡，有范宽之风。

TUNE: SILK-WASHING STREAM

— Yan Shu

A song filled with new words and a cup with old wine, the bower is last year's and the weather as fine. Will last year reappear as the sun on decline?

Deeply I sigh for the flowers fallen in vain; vaguely I seem to know the swallows come again. In fragrant garden path alone I still remain.

huàn xī shā

浣 溪 沙

yàn shū
—— 晏 殊

yì qǔ xīn cí jiǔ yì bēi qù nián
一 曲 新 词 酒 一 杯 , 去 年
tiān qì jiù tíng tái xī yáng xī xià jǐ shí
天 气 旧 亭 台 , 夕 阳 西 下 几 时
huí
回 ?
wú kě nài hé huā luò qù sì céng
无 可 奈 何 花 落 去 , 似 曾
xiāng shí yàn guī lái xiǎo yuán xiāng jìng dú pái
相 识 燕 归 来 。 小 园 香 径 独 徘
huái
徊 ① 。

注 释

① 香径：铺满落花的小路。徘徊：
来回走动。

28

Oranges, Grapes and Pomegranates by Lu Zonggui, Southern Song, album leaf, color on silk, 24 x 25.8 cm, kept in Boston Museum of Fine Arts, U.S.A. In a Chinese tradition, the theme of the painting is to have many sons and to have many blessings. Lu seldom put his signature to his works. In this picture, the painter's signature is dimly visible on the left above the pomegranate leaves.

◎ 橘子、葡萄、石榴图，鲁宗贵，册页，绢本设色，24 × 25.8cm，美国波士顿艺术博物馆藏。这是一幅有确切题款的南宋作品。画橘子、葡萄和石榴，象征多子多孙的美好愿望。用色精细、沉着，写实性极强。在左半部石榴叶上有不规则的"鲁宗贵"款署，题字极小，隐约可见。在流传下来的南宋作品中，很少有鲁宗贵题款的作品，此图殊为珍贵。

TUNE: SILK-WASHING STREAM

— Yan Shu

What can a short-lived man do with the fleeting year and soul-consuming separations from his dear? Refuse no banquet when fair singing girls appear!

With hills and rills in sight, I miss the far-off in vain. How can I bear the fallen blooms in wind and rain! Why not enjoy the fleeting pleasure now again?

注　释

①"一向"句：片刻的时光，有限的生命。一向，一晌，即一会儿。

②等闲：平常的，寻常的。

③"满目"句：放眼望去，山河满目，令人不由得感念起远方的亲人。

④"不如"句：作为宰相的作者本人不会沉迷于歌酒之中伤痛不能自拔，在当下的酒宴上，他会好好爱怜眼前与身边的歌女，及时行乐。

huǎn xī shā
浣 溪 沙

—— yàn shū
晏 殊

yī xiàng nián guāng yǒu xiàn shēn   děng
一 向 年 光 有 限 身 ①， 等

xián lí bié yì xiāo hún ②   jiǔ yàn gē xí
闲 离 别 易 销 魂 。 酒 宴 歌 席

mò cí pín
莫 辞 频 。

mǎn mù shān hé kōng niàn yuǎn ③   luò
满 目 山 河 空 念 远 ， 落

huā fēng yǔ gèng shāng chūn   bù rú lián qǔ yǎn
花 风 雨 更 伤 春 。 不 如 怜 取 眼

qián rén ④
前 人 。

Winter Birds by Cui Bai, Northern Song, handscroll, color on silk, 25.5 x 101.4 cm, kept in the Palace Museum of Beijing. It depicts a flock of sparrows perched on the branches of an ancient tree in a winter dusk. The composition is ingenious and well balanced, with the agile birds and spreading branches making a striking contrast.

◎ 寒雀图卷, 北宋, 崔白, 绢本设色, 25.5 × 101.4 cm, 北京故宫博物院藏。作品描绘隆冬的黄昏, 一群麻雀在古木上安栖入寐的景象。构图上动静有致、上下呼应、浑然一体, 鸟的灵动在此基础上被表现得维妙维肖。树干在形骨清秀的鸟雀衬托下, 显得格外混穆恬澹, 苍寒野逸。造型纯以墨法, 笔踪难寻。

TUNE: SPRING IN JADE PAVILION
SPRING GRIEF

— Yan Shu

Farewell Pavilion green with grass and willow trees! How could my gallant young lord have left me with ease! I'm woke by midnight bell from dim dream in my bower; parting grief won't part with flowers falling in shower.

My beloved feels not the grief my loving heart sheds: each string as woven with thousands of painful threads. However far and wide the sky and earth may be, they can't measure the lovesickness o'erwhelming me.

精选
宋词
与
宋画

注　释

① "绿杨"二句：写春天一个少妇思夫怨夫的情景。少妇于长亭送别她的丈夫，埋怨他少不更事，早早地将她抛弃，独自一人远去他乡。

② "无情"二句："多情的人"是少妇自称，比无情的人心底苦得多，一寸相思会因思之深切变成千万缕思念，萦绕心头。

yù lóu chūn
玉 楼 春

chūn hèn
春 恨

—— yàn shū
晏 殊

绿杨芳草长亭路，年少
抛人容易去①。楼头残梦五
更钟，花底离情三月雨。
无情不似多情苦，一寸
还成千万缕②。天涯地角有
穷时，只有相思无尽处。

32

Double Happiness, also known as *Two Jays and a Hare,* by Cui Bai, Northern Song, hanging scroll, color on silk, 193.7 x 103.4 cm, kept in the Palace Museum of Taipei. The painting's composition shows great originality. The artist placed two birds on the top right corner and a hare on the bottom left corner of the scroll, with an ancient tree stretching cater-cornered from bottom right to top left. The hare and birds were drawn with delicate strokes, while the tree, hillside and wilted grass with both fine and freehand brushwork.

◎ 双喜图轴，北宋，崔白，绢本设色，193.7 × 103.4cm，台北故宫博物院藏。此图又名《禽兔图》。绘秋风肃杀中，两只寒雀飞临于枯木槎桠，树下一只肥兔正引首回顾。秋兔双禽，高下对峙，互为呼应。画中以半工半写之法，绘枯木、衰草和山坡，兔禽则用工笔，刻画细致。色彩清淡，体现了前人所说的"体制清淡，作用疏通"的艺术特色。

TUNE: PURE SERENE MUSIC

— Yan Shu

On rosy paper a hand fair has laid the innermost heart bare. Nor fish below nor swan above would bear this melancholy message of love.

At sunset on west tower alone she stands still; the curtain hook can't hang up distant hill. Who knows where her beloved is gone? Green waves still eastward roll on.

qīng píng yuè
清平乐

yàn shū
—— 晏殊

hóng jiān xiǎo zì shuō jìn píng shēng yì hóng yàn zài yún yú zài shuǐ chóu chàng cǐ qíng nán jì
红笺小字①，说尽平生意。鸿雁在云鱼在水②，惆怅此情难寄。

xié yáng dú yǐ xī lóu yáo shān qià duì lián gōu rén miàn bù zhī hé chù lǜ bō yī jiù dōng liú
斜阳独倚西楼，遥山恰对帘钩③。人面不知何处④，绿波依旧东流。

注 释

①红笺：印有红格的绢纸，多指情书。

②鸿雁：大雁。

③帘钩：挂窗帘的铜钩，此代指窗户。

④人面：用“人面桃花”典故。

Bamboo by Wen Tong, Northern Song, hanging scroll, ink on silk, 131.6 x 105.4 cm, kept in the Palace Museum of Taipei. Wen was a painter famous for his ink bamboo paintings. He used rich ink to draw the obverse side of bamboo leaves and light ink for the reverse side. Wen along with Su Shi originated the Huzhou school, which had a far-reaching influence upon bamboo painters of later ages.

◎ 墨竹图轴，北宋，文同，绢本墨笔，131.6 × 105.4cm，台北故宫博物院藏。文同传派为湖洲竹派，影响深远，此图用水墨画倒垂竹枝，以独创深墨为面、淡墨为背之法写竹叶，浓淡相宜，张弛有致，其中灵气扑面而来。笔法谨严有致，又现潇洒之态。是写竹不可多得之佳品。

TUNE: SPRING IN JADE PAVILION

—Song Qi

The scenery is getting fine east of the town; the rippling water greets boats rowing up and down. Beyond green willows morning chill is growing mild; on pink apricot branches spring is running wild.

In our floating life scarce are pleasures we seek after. How can we value gold above a hearty laughter? I raise wine cup to ask the slanting sun to stay and leave among the flowers its departing ray.

yù lóu chūn
玉 楼 春

—— sòng qí
宋 祁

dōng chéng jiàn jué fēng guāng hǎo , hú zhōu
东 城 渐 觉 风 光 好 , 縠 绉

bō wén yíng kè zhào ① lǜ yáng yān wài xiǎo
波 纹 迎 客 棹 ① 。 绿 杨 烟 外 晓

hán qīng , hóng xìng zhī tóu chūn yì nào
寒 轻 , 红 杏 枝 头 春 意 闹 。

fú shēng cháng hèn huān yú shǎo ② kěn
浮 生 长 恨 欢 娱 少 ② , 肯

ài huáng jīn qīng yí xiào ③ wèi jūn chí jiǔ
爱 黄 金 轻 一 笑 ③ ? 为 君 持 酒

quàn xié yáng ④ qiě xiàng huā jiān liú wǎn zhào
劝 斜 阳 ④ , 且 向 花 间 留 晚 照 。

注 释

①縠绉:有皱纹的丝绸,形容波纹之细;棹:船桨。

②浮生:对人生的一种消极称谓,意指世事无定,人生短促。长:常。

③肯爱:肯,怎肯,反诘语气。爱,吝惜

④劝:敬酒。

Plum, Bamboo and Birds, author and size unknown, Southern Song, ink and wash, a private collection kept in the U.S.A. It's a representative work of the Southern Song imperial-court flower-and-bird painting. The composition, color and outlines are reminiscent of renowned court painter Lin Chun.

◎ 梅竹雀图，佚名，水墨设色，尺寸不详，美国私人收藏。此图体现了南宋院体花鸟画的典型特征。图中梅竹相依，由左向下斜势而出，枝头黄莺，宛然欲起，饶有生趣。构图之精巧，线条勾勒之细腻，设色之清疏淡雅，都与院体名家林椿的画风相近。

TUNE: SONG OF HAWTHORN

—Ouyang Xiu

Last year on lunar festive night, lanterns 'mid blooms shone as daylight. The moon rose atop willow tree; my lover had a tryst with me.

This year on lunar festive night, moon and lanterns still shine as bright. But where's my lover of last year? My sleeves are wet with tear on tear.

生查子
shēng zhā zǐ

—欧阳修
ōu yáng xiū

去年元夜时^①，花市灯
qù nián yuán yè shí　　　huā shì dēng

如昼。月上柳梢头，人约黄
rú zhòu　yuè shàng liǔ shāo tóu　rén yuē huáng

昏后。
hūn hòu

今年元夜时，月与灯依
jīn nián yuán yè shí　yuè yǔ dēng yī

旧。不见去年人，泪湿春衫
jiù　bú jiàn qù nián rén　lèi shī chūn shān

袖。
xiù

注 释

①元夜：正月十五，元宵之夜，又
称灯节。从唐代 (618—907) 起，
在元夜有观灯的风俗。

38

Children Playing in Autumn Courtyard by Su Hanchen, Southern Song, hanging scroll, color on silk, 197.5 x 108.7 cm, kept in the Palace Museum of Taipei. In the painting elder sister and younger brother are playing a game in which Chinese dates are pushed around on a round stool. The artist displayed his superb skill in sketching.

◎ 秋庭戏婴（局部），南宋，苏汉臣，绢本设色，197.5 × 108.7cm，台北故宫博物院藏。苏汉臣专长人物画，尤善描写儿童生活。画面上锦装玉琢的姐弟俩正头挨着头，弯身站在鼓凳旁，玩枣推磨的游戏。穿红衣的弟弟显然占了上风，正伸出小手，要继续出击，姐姐微微张口，仿佛要争辩。此画可见苏汉臣绘画其刻画入微的写生功底。

TUNE: SPRING IN JADE PAVILION

— Ouyang Xiu

In front of wine I'll tell you of my parting day; your vernal face dissolves in tears before I say. Lovers are born with sentimental feeling heart; nor moon nor wind has taken in their grief a part.

Don't set to a new tune the parting song! The old has tied our hearts in knots for long. Until we have seen all flowers on the trees, it's hard to bid goodbye to vernal breeze.

玉楼春

yù lóu chūn

— 欧阳修 *ōu yáng xiū*

尊前拟把归期说，欲语
zūn qián nǐ bǎ guī qī shuō　*yù yǔ*

春容先惨咽。人生自是有情
chūn róng xiān cǎn yè　*rén shēng zì shì yǒu qíng*

痴，此恨不关风与月。
chī　*cǐ hèn bù guān fēng yǔ yuè*

离歌且莫翻新阕，一曲
lí gē qiě mò fān xīn què　*yì qǔ*

能教肠寸结①。直须看尽洛
néng jiāo cháng cùn jié　*zhí xū kàn jìn luò*

城花，始共春风容易别②。
chéng huā　*shǐ gòng chūn fēng róng yì bié*

注　释

① "离歌" 二句：离别的歌不要再填新词了，这一曲便直教人肝肠寸结。

② "直须" 二句：离别时还是多在春风里看看洛阳城里的繁花，在欣欣向荣的春天里使得分离变得更容易一些。这是作者提醒对方不要太过伤感，须振作一些。

Jagged Rocks, Distant Landscape by Guo Xi, Northern Song, handscroll, color on silk, 120.8 x 167.7 cm, kept in the Palace Museum of Beijing. Guo carried on Li Cheng's tradition, and his painting was highly praised by Emperor Shenzong. This picture is one of Guo's representative works, in which he used powerful strokes to draw mountain rocks and withered trees, presenting a tranquil and secluded scene.

◎ 窠石平远图轴，北宋，郭熙，绢本设色，120.8 × 167.7cm，北京故宫博物院藏。郭熙继承了李成的画风，并因此受到宋神宗的推崇，其画风也极北宋画坛一时之盛，这幅《窠石平远图》是郭熙代表作之一。图中景物一般，但在画家的笔下，山石形如鬼面，瘦树枯枝苍劲有力，呈现出幽奇神奥的意味。

TUNE: BUTTERFLIES IN LOVE
WITH FLOWERS

—Ouyang Xiu

Deep, deep the courtyard where he is, so deep
it's veiled by smokelike willows heap on heap, by
curtain on curtain and screen on screen. Leaving his
saddle and bridle, there he has been merrymaking.
From my tower his trace can't be seen.

The third moon now, the wind and rain are rag-
ing late; at dusk I bar the gate, but I can't bar in spring.
My tearful eyes ask flowers, but they fail to bring an
answer, I see red blooms fly over the swing.

注　释

①无重数: 重重叠叠, 形容帘幕甚
多。
②玉勒: 镶玉的笼头。雕鞍: 雕有
花纹的马鞍。游冶处: 寻欢觅艳的
场所。
③章台路: 章台, 秦宫名, 在长安。
其下为章台街, 至汉犹存, 为妓女
聚居之所。
④雨横: 雨势暴猛。
⑤乱红: 指落花片片。

dié liàn huā
蝶 恋 花

—— ōu yáng xiū
欧 阳 修

tíng yuàn shēn shēn shēn jǐ xǔ   yáng liǔ duī
庭 院 深 深 深 几 许 ? 杨 柳 堆

yān   lián mù wú chóng shù ①   yù lè diāo ān
烟 , 帘 幕 无 重 数 。 玉 勒 雕 鞍

yóu yě chù ②   lóu gāo bū jiàn zhāng tái lù ③
游 冶 处 , 楼 高 不 见 章 台 路 。

yǔ hèng fēng kuáng sān yuè mù ④   mén yǎn
雨 横 风 狂 三 月 暮 , 门 掩

huáng hūn   wú jì liú chūn zhù   lèi yǎn wèn huā
黄 昏 , 无 计 留 春 住 。 泪 眼 问 花

huā bù yǔ   luàn hóng fēi guò qiū qiān qù ⑤
花 不 语 , 乱 红 飞 过 秋 千 去 。

42

Hibiscus, author unknown, Southern Song, round fan, color on silk, 25 x 26.2 cm, kept in the Palace Museum of Taipei. The unknown artist outlined the petals and leaves with ink lines. The painting with a simple composition is in delightful taste.

◎ 芙蓉图，佚名，团扇，绢本设色，25 × 26.2cm，中国台北故宫博物院藏。芙蓉有水、木之分，二者在中国的文人士大夫眼中，都是清雅秀洁之物，所以在诗文图画中皆有表现。这一幅画所绘为木芙蓉，构图简洁，花枝斜出，弯曲有致。花、叶皆以墨线勾勒轮廓，用笔流畅生动，敷彩清淡，有雅洁之妙。

精选

宋词与宋画

TUNE: SONG OF A SOUTHERN COUNTRY

— Wang Anshi

The capital's been ruled by kings since days gone by. The rich green and lush gloom breathe a majestic sigh. Like dreams has passed the reign of four hundred long years, which calls forth tears. Ancient laureates were buried like their ancient peers.

Along the river I go where I will; up city walls and watch towers I gaze my fill. Do not ask what has passed without leaving a trail! To what avail? The endless river rolls in vain beyond the rail.

注 释

①帝王州：指南京，南京曾为六朝故都。

②"晋代"句：指作为东晋故都的南京一带。如今东晋士大夫的丰功伟绩已如荒丘般被土所埋。词用李白《江上吟》诗意"屈平词赋悬日月，楚王台榭空山丘"。又借用李白《登金陵凤凰台》中原句，点明功名富贵不过是过眼云烟，不值得留连。

南乡子 (nán xiāng zǐ)

— 王安石 (wáng ān shí)

自古帝王州①，郁郁葱葱佳气浮。四百年来成一梦，堪愁。晋代衣冠成古丘②。

绕水恣行游，上尽层城更上楼。往事悠悠君莫问，回头。槛外长江空自流。

Mist-covered River and Undulating Mountains by Wang Shen, Northern Song, handscroll, color on silk, 45.2 x 166 cm, kept in Shanghai Museum. Range upon range of mountains undulate on both sides of a mist-covered river. In this painting the artist made a daring attempt to combine the literati painting and imperial-court decorative painting techniques.

◎ 烟江叠嶂图卷，北宋，王诜，绢本设色，45.2 × 166cm，上海博物馆藏。这是王诜水墨加青绿的混合画法的典型代表作。画幅上一片平远浩渺的空旷烟江，左边江心重峦叠嶂，笔法上虽还能看出李成的影响，但用笔更趋尖方，有明显的个人风格。其画法是在墨笔勾皴之后，先用淡墨、花青渲染，然后再用青绿罩染。这种画法，实际上是文人风格与院体风格相互融合的一种大胆尝试。

TUNE: PARTRIDGE IN THE SKY

— Yan Jidao

Time and again with rainbow sleeves you tried to fill my cup with wine that, drunk, I kept on drinking still. You danced till the moon hung low over the willow trees; you sang until amid peach blossoms blushed the breeze.

Then came the time to part, but you're deep in my heart. How many times have I met you in dreams at night! Now left to gaze at you in silver candlelight, I fear it is not you, but a sweet dream untrue.

鹧鸪天

—— 晏几道

彩袖殷勤捧玉钟①，当年拚却醉颜红②。舞低杨柳楼心月③，歌尽桃花扇影风④。

从别后，忆相逢，几回魂梦与君同！今宵剩把银釭照⑤，犹恐相逢是梦中。

注 释

①彩袖：彩色的衣服，歌女所穿，代指女子。玉钟：玉杯。

②拚却：甘愿、不顾之意。

③"舞低"句："低"字为使动用法。舞到月亮从楼心（天井）西沉，说明时间之长。

④"歌尽"句：歌扇的柔风渐渐渐灭，表明精力耗尽。

⑤剩把：尽把。银釭：银质灯台。

Crows on a Willow (partial) by Zhao Ji (Emperor Huizong), Northern Song, handscroll, light color on paper, 34 x 233 cm, kept in Shanghai Museum. The painter accurately portrayed the crows resting on a weeping willow that put forth new buds. Many very fine strokes of light color create an unperturbed and nonchalant effect.

◎ 柳鸦图卷（局部），北宋，宋徽宗赵佶，纸本淡设色，34 × 233cm，上海博物馆藏。此图中柳芽芦雁采用没骨画法，竹以双钩法绘出，设色浅淡，构图洗练。粗壮的柳根、细嫩的枝条、姿貌丰腴的栖鸦、芦雁画得都很精细工整。栖鸦双双憩息、嬉戏，芦雁饮水啄食，形态自在安详。点睛用生漆，更显得神采奕奕。整个画面恬静雅致、气静神闲。

TUNE: THE LOVER'S RETURN

— Yan Jidao

Old perfume and face powder smell as before; to my regret your love's no more. You sent me but few lines in spring, still fewer words does autumn bring.

Cold phoenix quilt for two, and lovebird pillow lonely, my sorrow can be drowned in wine only. E'en if I dream of you, the dream will not come true. Now you won't come in dreams, what can I do?

ruǎn láng gūi

阮 郎 归

— 晏几道

jiù xiāng cán fěn sì dāng chū   rén qíng
旧 香 残 粉 似 当 初 ，   人 情
hèn bù rú   yì chūn yóu yǒu shù háng shū
恨 不 如①。   一 春 犹 有 数 行 书 ，
qiū lái shū gèng shū
秋 来 书 更 疏②。

qīn fèng lěng   zhěn yuān gū   chóu cháng
衾 凤 冷 ， 枕 鸳 孤 ， 愁 肠
dài jiǔ shū   mèng hún zòng yǒu yě chéng xū
待 酒 舒③。   梦 魂 纵 有 也 成 虚 ，
nǎ kān hé mèng wú
那 堪 和 梦 无 ？

注 释

①"旧香"句：以物与人相比。往者所用香粉虽给人以残旧之感，但物仍故物，香犹故香，而离去之人的感情，却经不起空间与时间考验，逐渐淡薄，今不如昔了。

②"一春"句：是上两句的补充和延伸，举出人不如物不如昔的事实，那就是行人初去时还有几行书信寄来，从春到秋，书信越来越稀少了。

③"衾凤冷"句：衾枕本是无知物。被上绣的凤凰，枕上绣的鸳鸯也应仍"似当初"，当初是那样，现在也是那样，只是在独眠之人的眼中、心上产生了清冷、孤寂之感。

Reading Tablet Inscription Among Jagged Rocks, ascribed to Li Cheng, Northern Song, hanging scroll, ink on silk, 126.3 x 104.9 cm, kept in Osaka Municipal Art Museum, Japan. Li was a descendant of the Tang Dynasty's imperial family. Since childhood he studied Confucian classics, but owing to straitened family circumstances, throughout his life he never had a chance to get official position. Thus Li turned to painting to entertain himself. His paintings were appreciated by literati artists as they showed indifference to fame and fortune. And he was acclaimed in the Northern Song as "No.1 painter in history." After he died, Li left behind very few paintings. Though this scroll has been ascribed to him, its true authorship remains unknown. Nevertheless, the bleak scene as well as the author's nostalgia for the past expressed in this painting tallies with Li's style as recorded in historical materials.

◎ 读碑窠石图轴，北宋，李成（传），绢本墨笔，126.3×104.9cm，日本大阪市立美术馆藏。李成本是唐皇族后裔，至宋时家世已经没落不堪，虽然他自幼熟读经史，工于诗文，但却才命不遇，一生布衣。不得已，乃放意于诗酒，寓兴于画。因他的绘画原意只是自娱，所以在烟林清旷中能呈现出秀润不凡的气质，博得文人士大夫赞赏，在北宋时被誉为"古今第一"。他的传世作品很少，这一件《读碑窠石图》也只是传为他的作品而实不可考，但画面中传达出来的文人怀古幽思与萧疏气象，与记载中李成的画风是吻合一致的。

精选
宋词
与
宋画

TUNE: GATHERING MULBERRIES

— Yan Jidao

Since autumn came, my soul has been consumed for you, your letters still so few. At home or on the way, could we look at each other as in olden day?

In south tower we sate side by side, hand in hand, known to wind and moonbeams. But since you left the land, where could we sit again side by side but in dreams?

căi sāng zǐ
采桑子

——晏几道
yàn jī dào

秋来更觉销魂苦①，小字
qiū lái gèng jué xiāo hún kǔ　　　xiǎo zì
还稀②。坐想行思，怎得相看
hái xī　　　zuò xiǎng xíng sī　　　zěn dé xiāng kàn
似旧时？
sì jiù shí

南楼把酒凭肩处，风月
nán lóu bǎ jiǔ píng jiān chù　　fēng yuè
应知。别后除非，梦里时时
yīng zhī　　bié hòu chú fēi　　mèng lǐ shí shí
得见伊。
dé jiàn yī

注　释

①"秋来"句：意指与恋人分别后，自己独处的愁苦秋日。

②"小字"句：平生爱慕之意，应用密密麻麻的小字书写在红笺之上，此处反用其意，在于曲折表达作者思念离人悱恻缠绵之心境，欲写书笺传情达意，又无意绪，字迹之稀乃情之深所至。

50

Spinning Wheel by Wang Juzheng, Northern Song, handscroll, color on silk, 26.1 x 69.2 cm, kept in the Palace Museum of Beijing. Wang, a folk painter, knew well the hardships of the people living at the bottom of society. The picture portrays a mother and her daughter-in-law engaged in spinning.

◎ 纺车图卷，北宋，王居正，绢本设色，26.1 × 69.2 cm，北京故宫博物院藏。王居正是民间的画师，对民间生活有较深入体会。这一幅《纺车图》就是对民间家庭生活的描写。画面表现的是在纺车上倒线的婆媳二人，婆婆腰弯背驼，摇纺车的媳妇一边劳动，一手还抱着正吃奶的婴儿。

TUNE: TELLING INNERMOST FEELING

— Yan Jidao

I oft remember your robe when green grass is seen, perfumed by incense burnt your girdle green. All is quiet along the balustrade, on which we leaned when daylight began to fade.

The breeze is full of grace, the moon has left no trace, my soul is steeped in hidden grief. And I would try to write it on a withered flower or leaf and send it to the morning cloud on high.

sù zhōng qíng
诉 衷 情

—— 晏几道

长 因 蕙 草 记 罗 裙 ①，绿 腰
沉 水 熏 ②。阑 干 曲 处 人 静，曾
共 倚 黄 昏 。

风 有 韵 ，月 无 痕 ，暗 销
魂 。拟 将 幽 恨 ，试 写 残 花 ，寄
与 朝 云 。

注 释

①此句从朱希济《生查子》"记得绿罗裙，处处怜芳草"化出。蕙草，即兰草，香草。

②"绿腰"句：绿色的裙腰是用沉香熏过的。沉水，即沉香。又名水沉，一种香料。

Swaying Lotus Leaves in Taiye Pool, author unknown, Southern Song, round fan, color on silk, 23.8 x 25.1 cm, kept in the Palace Museum of Taipei. The picture portrays a beautiful summer landscape. A balmy breeze ripples blooming lotus flowers and lush green leaves. Wild ducks swim in the lotus pond, with butterflies and a newly hatched swallow flying above. It's an outstanding imperial-court decorative painting.

◎ 太液荷风图，佚名，团扇，绢本设色，23.8 × 25.1cm，中国台北故宫博物院藏。太液池内碧叶连天，莲花掩映，浮萍丛生，几对野鸭正倘佯于湖面之上；空中彩蝶飞舞，乳燕展翅，一派风和日丽的景色。叶、花皆双勾填彩，以色彩之深浅绘出仰俯向背的关系。用笔十分精细，得院体画之精髓。

TUNE: PRELUDE TO WATER MELODY

— Su Shi

How long will the full moon appear? Wine cup in hand, I ask the sky. I do not know what time of year it would be tonight in the palace on high. Riding the wind, there I would fly, yet I'm afraid the crystalline palace would be too high and cold for me. I rise and dance, with my shadow I play. On high as on earth, would it be as gay?

The moon goes round the mansions red through gauze-draped windows to shed her light upon the sleepless bed. Against man she should have no spite. Why then when people part, is she oft full and bright? Men have sorrow and joy, they meet or part again; the moon is bright or dim and she may wax or wane. There has been nothing perfect since the olden days. So let us wish that man may live long as he can! Though miles apart, we'll share the beauty she displays.

A Pair of Birds on Wintersweet by Zhao Ji (Emperor Huizong), Northern Song, album leaf, color on silk, 25.8 x 26.1 cm, kept in Sichuan Provincial Museum. A wintersweet spreads its branches apart, on which two birds are resting and yellow flowers are in blossom. The composition is simple, but lucid and lively.

◎ 腊梅双禽图页，北宋，宋徽宗赵佶，绢本设色，25.8 × 26.1cm，四川博物馆藏。此图中画一只腊梅，弯曲有致，枝梢有数朵梅花已然开放。两只山禽似被画面外的什么所吸引，正顾盼观望。画中彩墨工细，运用自如，细笔勾花、枝，设色清雅。山禽刻画细致，神情逼真。构图疏朗，明快大方。

水调歌头

—— 苏轼

明月几时有？把酒问青天。不知天上宫阙①，今夕是何年？我欲乘风归去，又恐琼楼玉宇②，高处不胜寒。起舞弄清影，何似在人间③！

转朱阁，低绮户④，照无眠。不应有恨，何事长向别时圆？人有悲欢离合，月有阴晴圆缺，此事古难全。但愿人长久，千里共婵娟⑤！

注　释

①宫阙：官殿。官门两侧的楼观叫阙。

②琼楼玉宇：神仙楼馆。琼：美玉。

③何似：何如。

④绮户：镂花的窗户。

⑤婵娟：美女之称。这里指月亮。

Whispering Pines in the Mountains by Li Tang, Northern Song, hanging scroll, color on silk, 188.7 x 139.8 cm, kept in the Palace Museum of Taipei. In this scroll, the valley in the foreground is overgrown with pine trees, while rocky peaks in the distance thrust themselves toward the sky. Interestingly, the painter inscribed his name above the distant peaks, which shows great originality.

◎ 万壑松风图卷，北宋，李唐，绢本设色，188.7 × 139.8cm，台北故宫博物院藏。在这幅画中，群松杂簇于壑内，两边山石突兀丛叠，远峰似剑直入云天，飞瀑直泻而下，汇入河谷，奔流画外。山石坚实，树木丰茂，意境清凉、幽静，造成一种湿重的空气扑面而来的强烈感觉。别有意趣的是，这幅画中的题款书写在远山的山峰上，可算是李唐的匠心独运了。

TUNE: CHARM OF A MAIDEN SINGER

— Su Shi

The endless river eastward flows; with its huge waves are gone all those gallant heroes of bygone years. West of the ancient fortress appears Red Cliff where General Zhou won his early fame when the Three Kingdoms were in flame. Rocks tower in the air and waves beat on the shore, rolling up a thousand heaps of snow. To match the land so fair, how many heroes of yore had made great show!

I fancy General Zhou at the height of his success, with a plume fan in hand, in a silk hood, so brave and bright, laughing and jesting with his bride so fair, while enemy ships were destroyed as planned like castles in the air. Should their souls revisit this land, sentimental, his bride would laugh to say: Younger than they, I have my hair turned grey. Life is but like a dream. O moon, I drink to you who have seen them on the stream.

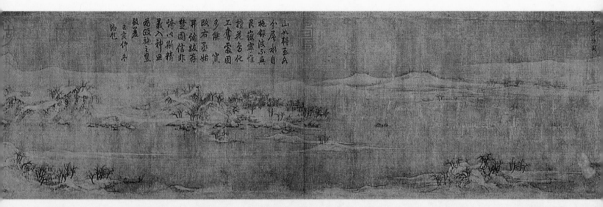

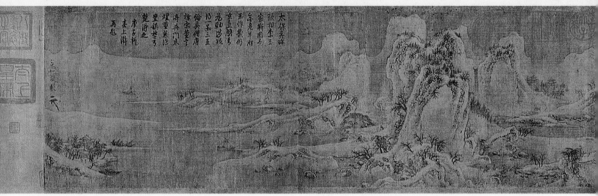

Returning Boat on Snow-covered River, ascribed to Zhao Ji (Emperor Huizong), Northern Song, handscroll, color on silk, 30.3 x 190.8 cm, kept in the Palace Museum of Beijing. Many Northern Song paintings bear the signature of Zhao Ji, but considering their inconsistent styles, a lot might not be made in his own hand. This picture depicts a world of ice and snow, but overflowing with vigor. It's hard to judge if it is Zhao's personal work.

◎ 雪江归棹图卷，北宋，宋徽宗赵佶，绢本设色，30.3 × 190.8cm，北京故宫博物院藏。目前我们所能见到的宋代传世之作，有不少都题有宋徽宗赵佶的署名，但实际上恐怕不一定都是他亲笔之作，因为这些作品往往在风格上有较大的变化。这一幅《雪江归棹图》，是否是徽宗亲笔殊难料定，但能在冰天雪地之中表现出一股盎然的生机，却是难能可贵。

念奴娇

—— 苏轼

大江东去①，浪淘尽千古风流人物。故垒西边，人道是三国周郎赤壁②，乱石崩云，惊涛裂岸，卷起千堆雪。江山如画，一时多少豪杰！

遥想公瑾当年，小乔初嫁了③，雄姿英发④。羽扇纶巾⑤，谈笑间樯橹灰飞烟灭⑥。故国神游⑦，多情应笑我早生华发。人间如梦，一尊还酹江月⑧。

注 释

①大江: 长江。

②故垒: 古代的营垒。周郎: 周瑜,字公瑾,人称周郎。赤壁之战中,为吴兵统帅。

③小乔: 周瑜之妻,著名美人。

④英发: 英气勃勃。

⑤羽扇纶巾: 儒将的装束。纶巾: 一种配有青色丝带的便帽。

⑥樯橹: 指战船。桅杆曰樯,桨曰橹。

⑦故国神游: 追想昔时的战况。故国: 指旧战场。

⑧酹: 烧酒祭奠,凭吊之意。

Red Cliff (*Chibi*) by Qiao Zhongchang, Northern Song, handscroll, ink on paper, size unknown, kept in the Nelson-Atkins Museum of Art, U.S.A. Qiao was a painter living at the terminal stage of the Northern Song Dynasty, and this is his only painting left behind. In the scroll he showed the shades and texture of trees, rocks and mountains by light-ink or dry-brush strokes, a method not commonly adopted until the following Yuan Dynasty.

◎ 赤壁图卷，北宋，乔中常，纸本墨笔，美国纳尔逊－艾金斯美术馆藏。乔仲常为北宋晚期人，生平经历均已失考，画迹也仅存此一幅。从作品中看来，这幅作品最大的价值在于，画中山石树木的笔法中出现了前所未见的干笔皴擦的技法。这种画法直到元代才为画家们大量运用，宋人作品中极为罕见。仅此一端，也可看出乔仲常在绘画上的探索精神了。

精选 宋词 与 宋画

TUNE: CALMING WIND AND WAVES

— Su Shi

Listen not to the rain beating against the trees.
Why don't you slowly walk and chant with ease?
Better than saddled horse I like sandals and cane.
Oh, I would fain, in a straw cloak, spend my life
in mist and rain.

Drunk, I am sobered by vernal wind shrill and
rather chill. In front I see the slanting sun atop the
hill; turning my head, I find the dreary beaten
track. Let me go back!Impervious to wind, rain or
shine, I'll have my will.

dìng fēng bō
定 风 波

—— sū shì
苏 轼

mò tīng chuān lín dǎ yè shēng hé fáng yín xiāo
莫 听 穿 林 打 叶 声 ， 何 妨 吟 啸

qiě xú xíng① zhú zhàng máng xié qīng shèng mǎ② shuí
且 徐 行①。 竹 杖 芒 鞋 轻 胜 马②， 谁

pà yì suō yān yǔ rèn píng shēng③
怕 ？ 一 蓑 烟 雨 任 平 生③。

liào qiào chūn fēng chuī jiǔ xǐng wēi lěng shān
料 峭 春 风 吹 酒 醒 ， 微 冷 。 山

tóu xié zhào què xiāng yíng huí shǒu xiàng lái xiāo sè
头 斜 照 却 相 迎 。 回 首 向 来 萧 瑟

chù guī qù yě wú fēng yǔ yě wú qíng
处 ， 归 去 ！ 也 无 风 雨 也 无 晴 。

注 释

①吟啸：在林中边吟诵诗句边寄
怀舒啸。
②"一蓑"句：因渔翁披蓑带笠于
江上，作者羡慕其自由潇洒的生
活态度，故称。

62

A *Thousand Li of Rivers and Mountains* (partial) by Wang Ximeng, Northern Song, handscroll, color on silk, 51.5 x 1191.5 cm, kept in the Palace Museum of Beijing. Legend goes that Wang, a young court painter, died soon after he finished this monumental work of art at age 18. It is a breathtakingly beautiful blue-and-green landscape panorama. In the scroll there is such a great variety of sights -- ships on the great river, undulating mountains, waterfalls, forests, villages, bridges and pavilions -- that one cannot take them all in with his or her eyes.

◎ 千里江山图卷（局部），北宋，王希孟，绢本设色，51.5 × 1191.5cm，北京故宫博物院藏。相传，王希孟18岁时完成这件作品后不久即死去，此作也就成为他的绘画绝唱。此作大青绿着色，染天染水，富丽细腻，画中山川江河交流展现，点缀以飞瀑流泉，丛林嘉树，庄园茅舍，舟楫桥亭，令人目不暇接，代表了画院青绿一体精密不苟、严格遵依格法的画风。

TUNE: BUTTERFLIES IN LOVE WITH FLOWERS

— Su Shi

Red flowers fade, green apricots appear still small, when swallows pass over blue water that surrounds the garden wall. Most willow catkins have been blown away, alas! But there is no place where grows no sweet grass.

Without the wall there is a path, within a swing. A passer-by hears a fair maiden's laughter in the garden ring. The ringing laughter fades to silence by and by; for the enchantress the enchanted can only sigh.

注　释

①褪：减退。

②天涯：天边。据《林下词谈》：苏轼贬惠州（广东惠阳）时曾令朝云歌唱此词，事在绍圣三年（1096）。则"天涯"为实指，非泛语。

③"多情"句：指多情的行人被佳人无心之笑所撩拨，而招致许多烦恼。

dié liàn huā
蝶恋花

— sū shì
苏轼

huā tuì cán hóng qīng xìng xiǎo ①, yàn zǐ
花　褪　残　红　青　杏　小　，　燕　子
fēi shí, lǜ shuǐ rén jiā rào。 zhī shàng liǔ mián
飞　时，　绿　水　人　家　绕。　枝　上　柳　棉
chuī yòu shǎo, tiān yá hé chù wú fāng cǎo ②!
吹　又　少，　天　涯　何　处　无　芳　草　！

qiáng lǐ qiū qiān qiáng wài dào, qiáng wài xíng
墙　里　秋　千　墙　外　道，　墙　外　行
rén, qiáng lǐ jiā rén xiào。 xiào jiàn bù wén shēng
人，　墙　里　佳　人　笑。　笑　渐　不　闻　声
jiàn qiāo, duō qíng què bèi wú qíng nǎo ③。
渐　悄，　多　情　却　被　无　情　恼　。

64

Cherry-apple Blossoms and Butterflies, author unknown, Southern Song, album leaf, color on silk, 25 x 24.5 cm, kept in the Palace Museum of Beijing. In this picture the unknown artist applied rich colors and fine touches to portray the flowers and leaves that whirl about in the wind.

◎ 海棠蛱蝶图，南宋，无款，绢本设色，25 × 24.5cm，北京故宫博物院藏。工笔重彩海棠花蝶，以叶花翻卷之状，将无形之风绘出，以"有形"写"无形"，十分精妙。此图用笔工整，敷色浓丽沉稳，花叶用颜色层层渲染出阴阳向背来，生动传神。

TUNE: RIVERSIDE TOWN

A DREAM ON THE NIGHT OF THE
20TH DAY OF THE 1ST MOON 1075

— Su Shi

For ten long years the living of the dead knows nought, though to my mind not brought, could the dead be forgot? Her lonely grave is far, a thousand miles away. To whom can I my grief convey? Revived even if she be, could she still know me? My face is worn with care, and frosted is my hair.

Last night I dreamed of coming to my native place; she was making up her face before her mirror with grace. Each saw the other hushed, but from our eyes tears gushed.Can I not be heart-broken when I am awoken from her grave clad with pines, where only the moon shines!

Early Spring by Guo Xi, Northern Song, hanging scroll, ink on silk, 158.3 x 108.1 cm, kept in the Palace Museum of Taipei. Guo imitated Li Cheng's style and expressed his unique feeling toward nature in his landscape painting. In this picture the artist of shrewd observation minutely depicted the changing scenery as spring is returning to the Earth.

◎ 早春图轴，北宋，郭熙，绢本墨笔，158.3×108.1cm，台北故宫博物院藏。郭熙作画，虽师法李成，却能博采众长，直抒胸意，特别是对山川自然有着敏锐的感受，能描绘出云烟出没峰峦隐显之态。这幅《早春图》敏锐地画出冬去春来、大地复苏的细致变化，山间雾气浮动，阳光和煦，穿插以行旅待渡等活动，传达出欣欣向荣的感情。

江城子

乙卯正月二十日夜记梦 ①

——苏轼

十年生死两茫茫 ②，不思量，自难忘。千里孤坟，无处话凄凉。纵使相逢应不识 ③，尘满面，鬓如霜。

夜来幽梦忽还乡，小轩窗 ④，正梳妆。相顾无言，唯有泪千行。料得年年肠断处，明月夜，短松冈 ⑤。

注 释

①这是苏东坡怀念亡妻的词，写于一场梦境以后。

②十年生死：轼妻王弗卒于志平二年（1065），至此整十年。归葬眉山故里，所以下文有"千里孤坟"之语。

③"纵使"句：因妻子亡故多年，纵使梦中相见，应该也不会相识。妻子的面容已经模糊难辨，何况她已离开人间，也不一定会认得尘埃满面，鬓发如霜的我呢。

④小轩窗：外有走廊的小窗户。轩：廊槛。

⑤短松冈：指栽着矮松的墓地。

Withered Tree and Queer Rock by Su Shi, Northern Song, handscroll, ink on paper. Very few of Su's paintings have been handed down to this very day. This scroll can be thought as his authentic work as it was mentioned in both Mi Fu and Liu Liangzuo's poems. A queer rock lies at the root of a withered tree with curled branches. Su spent years in official circles where schemes and intrigues were a common occurrence. In this picture he gave vent to his pent-up grief and indignation by describing the desolate scenery.

◎ 枯木怪石图卷，北宋，苏轼，纸本墨笔。大文豪苏轼的画迹，鲜少传世，此图因米芾、刘良佐等人的诗中有论及，所以可确认为苏轼的真迹。画面作老干虬枝的枯树一株，其形坚硬拙顽。树根处，以枯散旋转的笔锋皴出一块怪石，几片稀疏的篁叶从石后露出，画面意境沉郁悲凉。苏轼终生都处于官场的倾轧之中，故而性格傲岸颓放，常常发之于诗词书画，此图正是他表现内心郁结的典型作品。

TUNE: SONG OF DIVINATION

—Li Zhiyi

I live upstream and you downstream. From night to night of you I dream. Unlike the stream you're not in view, though we both drink from River Blue.

When will the water no more flow? When will my grief no longer grow? I wish your heart would be like mine, then not in vain for you I pine.

注 释

①"我住"句：一住江头，一住江尾，双方空间距离悬隔，也暗寓相思之情的悠长。

②"日日思君"句：江头江尾的万里遥隔，而同住长江之滨则引出了"共饮长江水"。尽管思而不见，毕竟还能共饮长江之水。

③"此水几时休"句：几时：何时。已：罢休。悠悠长江水，既是双方万里阻隔的天然障碍，又是一脉相通，遥寄情思的天然载体；既是悠悠相思，无穷别恨的触发物与象征，又是双方永恒相爱与期待的见证。

bǔ suàn zǐ
卜 算 子

—— lǐ zhī yí
李 之 仪

wǒ zhù cháng jiāng tóu   jūn zhù cháng jiāng
我 住 长 江 头 ， 君 住 长 江

wěi ①   rì rì sī jūn bú jiàn jūn   gòng yǐn
尾 。 日 日 思 君 不 见 君 ， 共 饮

cháng jiāng shuǐ ②
长 江 水 。

cǐ shuǐ jǐ shí xiū   cǐ hèng hé rì
此 水 几 时 休 ？ 此 恨 何 日

yǐ   zhǐ yuàn jūn xīn sì wǒ xīn   dìng bù
已 ？ 只 愿 君 心 似 我 心 ， 定 不

fù xiāng sī yì ③
负 相 思 意 。

Plum, Bamboo and Two Birds, author unknown, Southern Song, album leaf, color on silk, 26 x 26.5 cm, kept in the Palace Museum of Beijing. A pair of birds perches on plum branches in a verdant bamboo forest. The artist's style is similar to that of imperial-court decorative painters, which is exquisite but vivacious as well.

◎ 梅竹双雀图，佚名，册页，绢本设色，26 × 26.5cm，北京故宫博物院藏。此图绘绿竹丛中，白梅二枝，枝疏花茂，袅娜清冷。枝上两只小鸟栖息，其中一只抬头向上远眺，一只低头俯视，形神毕肖，茸毛质感逼真。图中竹叶为双钩填色，笔力劲辣，用笔精工，设色清丽。画风近于南宋画院一派，精工巧立中又见生动。

71

TUNE: CALMING WIND AND WAVES

— Huang Tingjian

The rain pours down for miles and miles in western land; all the day long like boats in water houses stand. When comes the Mountain-Climbing Day the weather's fine. Be drunk with wine in front of River Shu where Hell is near at hand.

Don't laugh at an old man still proud and in high glee! Oh, let us see how many white-haired heads are pinned with golden flower? I'd follow ancient poets at the Racing Tower. Let's shoot and ride! I'd tap them on the shoulder when we're side by side.

注　释

①黔中：郡名，唐置，后改黔州，宋升为绍庆府。治所在今四川彭水。漏天：连雨不止，像天漏了一样。

②重阳：旧历九月九日为重阳节。霁：指雨过天晴。

③鬼门关：即石门关，在四川奉节县东，两山相夹如门，故名。陆游《入蜀记》："舟中望石门关，仅通一人行，天下至险也。"蜀江：指流经彭水的乌江。

④气岸：气概轩昂。

⑤华颠：花白的头发。

⑥戏马台：项羽所筑，高八丈，广数百步，在今江苏铜山县南。东晋末年，刘裕北征过此。重阳节登台大宴僚佐，赋诗为乐。当时著名的诗人谢瞻、谢灵运俱有所作，"二谢"指此。

⑦风流犹拍古人肩：即可与古人媲美的意思。

dìng fēng bō
定 风 波

huāng tíng jiān
—— 黄 庭 坚

wàn lǐ qián zhōng yí lòu tiān　　　wū jū zhōng
万 里 黔 中 一 漏 天 ①， 屋 居 终
rì sì chéng chuán　　jí zhì chōng yáng tiān yě jì ②
日 似 乘 船 。 及 至 重 阳 天 也 霁 ，
cuī zuì　　guǐ mén guān wài shǔ jiāng qián ③
催 醉 ， 鬼 门 关 外 蜀 江 前 。

mò xiào lǎo wēng yóu qì àn ④　　jūn
莫 笑 老 翁 犹 气 岸 ， 君
kàn　　jǐ rén huáng jú shàng huā diān ⑤　　xì mǎ
看 ， 几 人 黄 菊 上 华 颠 ？ 戏 马
tái nán zhuī liǎng xiè ⑥　　chí shè　　fēng liú yóu
台 南 追 两 谢 ， 驰 射 ， 风 流 犹
pāi gǔ rén jiān ⑦
拍 古 人 肩 。

72

View from a Mountain Pavilion by Xiao Zhao, Southern Song, hanging scroll, ink and wash on silk, 179.3 x 112.7 cm, kept in the Palace Museum of Taipei. This is one of Xiao's enduring works. A pupil of Li Tang, he tended to depict the nation's magnificent and enchanting mountains and rivers in a solemn way to indirectly express his patriotic spirit.

◎ 山腰楼观图轴，南宋，萧照，绢本水墨画，179.3 × 112.7cm，台北故宫博物院藏。萧照是李唐的学生，除了效法他的老师在作品中表现有一定内容的人物画以外，也学习老师以山水画形式间接地表述一定的爱国精神的山水画。所以，他的山水画侧重于描绘山河的雄伟壮丽、坚定沉毅的形貌。这件作品是他的传世之作，画法酷似李唐，以坚硬的笔触作"小斧劈皴"，画法凝重。

TUNE: IMMORTALS AT THE MAGPIE BRIDGE

— Qin Guan

Clouds float like works of art, stars shoot with grief at heart. Across the Milky Way the Cowherd meets the Maid. When Autumn's Golden Wind embraces Dew of Jade, all the love scenes on earth, however many, fade.

Their tender love flows like a stream; their happy date seems but a dream. How can they bear a separate homeward way? If love between both sides can last for aye, why need they stay together night and day?

注 释

①纤云弄巧: 纤细的云彩, 就像织女在表现编织云棉的技巧一样。这里暗点节令。七夕, 阴历七月七日, 又称乞巧节, 妇女们向织女星祈祷, 请求传授刺绣缝纫的技巧。

②飞星传恨: 夜空的流星, 像是传递着牛郎和织女相思的苦恨。

③银汉: 银河。暗渡: 指牛郎织女深夜过桥幽会。

④金风: 秋风。玉露: 晶莹的露珠。

⑤佳期: 指情侣的会面。

⑥忍顾: 怎忍回头看。鹊桥: 传说每年七夕, 喜鹊架成长桥, 供牛郎织女渡银河相聚。

⑦朝朝暮暮: 指日夜相聚。

鹊桥仙
què qiáo xiān

—— 秦观
qín guān

纤 云 弄 巧 ①, 飞 星 传 恨 ②,
xiān yún nòng qiǎo　　　fēi xīng chuán hèn

银 汉 迢 迢 暗 渡 ③。 金 风 玉 露 一
yín hàn tiáo tiáo àn dù　　　jīn fēng yù lù yī

相 逢 ④, 便 胜 却 人 间 无 数 。
xiāng féng　　　biàn shèng què rén jiān wú shù

柔 情 似 水 , 佳 期 如 梦 ⑤,
róu qíng sì shuǐ　　　jiā qī rú mèng

忍 顾 鹊 桥 归 路 ⑥? 两 情 若 是 久
rěn gù què qiáo guī lù　　　liǎng qíng ruò shì jiǔ

长 时 , 又 岂 在 朝 朝 暮 暮 ⑦?
cháng shí　　　yòu qǐ zài zhāo zhāo mù mù

74

Frosty Bamboo and Winter Birds, author unknown, Southern Song, album leaf, color on silk, 26 x 26.5 cm, kept in the Palace Museum of Beijing. Five sparrows perch on withered thorny twigs with thin bamboos standing on the right. The unknown artist vividly portrayed the looks and motion of the birds.

◎ 霜筱寒雏图，册页，佚名，绢本设色，26 × 26.5cm，北京故宫博物院藏。图中绘五只麻雀栖止于枯棘上，左侧衬小竹槁枝，清韵冷翠。图中小鸟神态各异，动静不一，取向不同，形象生动逼真。从画面上看，小鸟的形象更接近自然情态，说明画家有敏锐的观察力和扎实的写实功力。此图用笔精工，设色优美。

TUNE: TREADING ON GRASS
AT AN INN OF CHENZHOU
— Qin Guan

Bowers are lost in mist; ferry dimmed in moonlight. Peach Blossom Land ideal is beyond the sight. Shut up in lonely inn, can I bear the cold spring? I hear at lengthening sunset homebound cuckoos sing.

Mume blossoms sent by friends and letters brought by post, nostalgic thoughts uncounted assail me oft in host. The lonely river flows around the lonely hill. Why should it southward flow, leaving me sad and ill?

注 释

①郴州：今湖南郴县。
②雾失楼台：浓雾遮住了楼台。
③月迷津渡：夜月迷忙，辨不清渡口。
④桃源：武陵（今湖南常德）有桃花源，即桃潜在《桃花源记》里所虚构的世外乐园。秦观南贬时路过桃源，曾做《点绛唇》词，表示了对理想仙境的向往。
⑤可堪：哪堪。
⑥杜鹃：又名子规。啼声凄切，如唤"不如归去"，容易勾起旅人的乡思。
⑦驿寄梅花：指亲友的寄赠。
⑧鱼传尺素：远方来信。古乐府《饮马长城窟行》："客从远方来，遗我双鲤鱼。呼童烹鲤鱼，中有尺素书。"尺素：古人以素绢为信笺，长约一尺，故名尺素。
⑨幸自：本自，本来。
⑩潇湘：湘水北流至湖南零陵县西与潇水会合，亦称潇湘。为谁：为什么。

踏莎行
郴州客舍①
—— 秦观

雾失楼台②，月迷津渡③，桃源望断无寻处④。可堪孤馆闭春寒⑤，杜鹃声里斜阳暮⑥。

驿寄梅花⑦，鱼传尺素⑧，砌成此恨无重数。郴江幸自绕郴山⑨，为谁流下潇湘去⑩！

76

Monkeys Picking Fruits, author unknown, Song Dynasty, album leaf, color on silk, 28.2 x 28.7 cm, kept in the Palace Museum of Beijing. In a virgin forest, three monkeys climb up a big tree. Two are eating fruits while playing; the other uses its right hand to cling to a branch while stretching out the left hand to pick fruits. The unknown artist portrayed agile and lively monkeys as well as curled branches with fine, delicate strokes.

◎ 猿猴摘果图，佚名，册页，绢本设色，28.2 × 28.7cm，北京故宫博物院藏。此图绘深山野林中，三只猿猴攀接栖止于树枝上。其中两猿正品果嬉戏，另一猿右臂抓树，左臂抓取红果，形象生动可爱。画家运用极为工细的笔法，描绘猿猴茸茸的细毛、灵巧的动态以及老树的虬枝和枯叶，显示出深厚功力。图中坡石用小斧劈皴，枝叶用双钩填色，笔法精工巧丽。

TUNE: COURTYARD FULL OF FRAGRANCE

— Qin Guan

A belt of clouds girds mountains high, and withered grass spreads to the sky. The painted horn at the watchtower blows. Before my boat sails up, let's drink a farewell cup. How many things which I recall of bygone days, one and all, all and one, are lost in mist and haze! Above the setting sun I see but dots of crows; around a lonely village water flows.

I'd call to mind the soul-consuming hours when I took off her perfume purse unseen, and loosened her silk girdle in her bower. All this has merely won me in the Mansion Green the name of a fickle lover. Now I'm a rover, O when can I see her again? My tears are shed in vain; in vain they wet my sleeves. It grieves my heart to find her bower out of sight, lost at dusk in city light.

Monkeys by Fa-chang, Southern Song, hanging scroll, ink and wash on silk, 173.9 x 98.8 cm, kept in Daitokuji Temple in Kyoto, Japan. Hanging on the right, it comprises a trio of wall scrolls along with *Guanyin* (C) and *Crane* (L). In the painting a mother monkey and her baby sit in an old pine tree. Using rich ink to depict their bodies while outlining their faces with a few strokes, this work of art gives a life-like portrayal of the two monkeys. The composition shows great originality with the tree stretching cater-cornered to soar into the skies.

◎ 猿图，法常，立轴，绢本水墨，173.9×98.8cm，日本京都大德寺藏。此图是和《鹤图》、《观音图》为三幅一套的右轴画。画中子母猿居于古松之上，猿与松的横斜交叉恰好平衡，且与中轴相连。笔法粗犷放达，猿周身浓黑、面部作白，五官用焦墨简点，近似符号，用墨画猿骨干、脚爪，后用笔擦之，质感很强。以"蔗渣草结"笔法写松干枝叶，不拘一格、生动泼辣。构图颇具匠心，松干由近及远，直插天空。附枝短权，使空间分割多样。

mǎn tíng fāng
满庭芳

qín guān
——秦观

shān mǒ wēi yún, tiān zhān shuāi cǎo, huà
山抹微云，天粘衰草①，画

jiǎo shēng duàn qiáo mén. zàn tíng zhēng zhào, liáo
角声断谯门②。暂停征棹③，聊

gòng yǐn lí zūn. duō shǎo péng lái jiù shì,
共饮离尊④。多少蓬莱旧事⑤，

kōng huí shǒu, yān ǎi fēn fēn. xié yáng wài,
空回首，烟霭纷纷。斜阳外，

hán yā shù diǎn, liú shuǐ rào gū cūn.
寒鸦数点，流水绕孤村⑥。

xiāo hún, dāng cǐ jì, xiāng náng àn
销魂⑦，当此际，香囊暗

jiě, luó dài qīng fēn. màn yíng dé qīng
解⑧，罗带轻分⑨。谩赢得青

lóu bó xìng míng cún. cǐ qù hé shí jiàn
楼薄悻名存⑩。此去何时见

yě, jīn xiù shàng, kōng rě tí hén. shāng qíng
也，襟袖上，空惹啼痕。伤情

chù, gāo lóu wàng duàn, dēng huǒ yǐ huáng hūn.
处，高楼望断，灯火已黄昏。

注释

①天粘衰草：远处的枯草紧贴着天际。粘，一作“连”。

②画角：绘以彩画的号角。谯门：城楼。下有门以通行人，上有楼以察敌情。这句说，城楼上的号角声已停歇，表示时已黄昏。

③征棹：远征的船。

④尊：同樽，酒杯。

⑤蓬莱旧事：秦观曾来绍兴蓬莱阁游冶，这里指对此地歌女留有恋情的往事。蓬莱：传说中的海上仙山。

⑥此两句从隋炀帝“寒鸦千万点，流水绕孤村”句化出。

⑦销魂：形容因悲伤或快乐而心神恍惚的样子。

⑧香囊：装香物的小囊，古人佩在身上的一种装饰物。

⑨罗带：丝织的带子。轻分：轻轻解下。

⑩谩：徒然。青楼：指妓女的住处。薄悻：薄情。

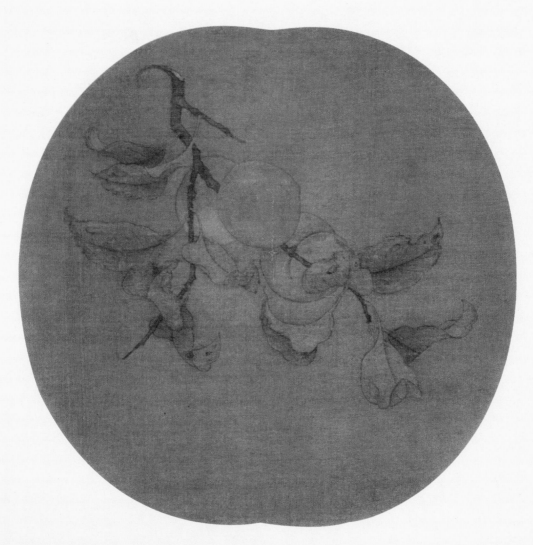

Peaches by Zhao Chang, Northern Song, round fan, color on silk, 27.5 x 29 cm, a private collection kept in Japan. Zhao regarded drawing from nature as important and was good at painting flowers and fruits. In this picture he drew peaches and leaves in graceful lines, rich colors and well-distributed running ink.

◎ 桃图，赵昌，绢本设色，27.5 × 29cm，日本私人藏。赵昌重视写生，自号"写生赵昌"。擅画花果，多作折枝化，兼工草虫。此图画折枝桃，枝叶多姿，桃形圆满，布局得当。勾线柔细，稍有浓淡变化，设色明丽，晕染均匀。

TUNE: SPRING IN PAINTED HALL

— Qin Guan

Lanes paved with fallen reds, the pool's full to the brim; in drizzling rain the sunrays swim. The apricot garden languishes with cuckoos' cries. What can I do when away spring flies?

I mount alone the willow-shaded tower, leaning on rails, my hand plays with a flower. Silent, I let it go when sunset glows. Who knows my grief? Who knows?

huà táng chūn
画 堂 春

—— qín guān
秦 观

luò hóng pū jìng shuǐ píng chí   nòng qíng
落 红 铺 径 水 平 池 ，   弄 晴

xiǎo yǔ fēi fēi ①   xìng yuán qiáo cuì dù juān
小 雨 霏 霏 。   杏 园 憔 悴 杜 鹃

tí   wú nài chūn guī
啼 ，   无 奈 春 归 。

liǔ wài huà lóu dú shàng   píng lán shǒu
柳 外 画 楼 独 上 ，   凭 栏 手

niǎn huā zhī   fàng huā wú yǔ duì xié huī ②
捻 花 枝 。   放 花 无 语 对 斜 晖 ，

cǐ hèn shuí zhī
此 恨 谁 知 ？

注 释

① "落红"二句：描述了暮春时节庭院小径中满地落红，小雨霏霏天欲晴，春池水涨的景象。
② 此句写原本捻花枝的手将花枝放开了，心事重重的她，无语对斜阳的情景。

Sketch of Butterflies by Zhao Chang, Northern Song, handscroll, color on paper, 27.7 x 91 cm, kept in the Palace Museum of Beijing. The sketch's composition shows great originality. The artist grouped brambles, wild flowers and bending reed in the painting's lower part in graceful disorder. The blank space intentionally left in the upper is dotted with several fluttering butterflies. It displays the painter's superb skill in painting.

◎ 写生蛱蝶图，赵昌，纸本设色，27.7 × 91cm，北京故宫博物院藏。这是描写秋天野外风物的写生画。在构图布局上，画家有意在画面上方留下很大的空白，景物多集中在画面的下部。将野菊、霜叶、荆棘和偃伏的芦苇等，布置得错落有致，并呈现出一种高旷清新、风物宜人的气质。作品用笔道劲有力，设色清丽典雅，花卉用笔简率，变化自然，蝴蝶、蚱蜢也各具质感，充分展示了"写生赵昌"高超的绘画技巧。

TUNE: SONG OF A FAIR MAIDEN

MIDNIGHT SONG

— He Zhu

The moon at midnight shines in mid-court on pear blossoms white. Pear blossoms white can't stand the flood of cuckoos' tears and blood.

My lord, why should no message come from you? The mulberries-shaded lanes have swallowed our adieu. Swallowed our adieu, the water seems to sob in streams.

yì qín é

忆秦娥

zǐ yè gē

子夜歌

hè zhù

——贺铸

sān gēng yuè, zhōng tíng qià zhào lí huā xuě。lí huā xuě, bū shēng qī duàn, dù juān tí xuě①。

三更月，中庭恰照梨花雪。梨花雪，不胜凄断，杜鹃啼血①。

wáng sūn hé xǔ yīn chén jué, róu sāng mò shàng tūn shēng bié。tūn shēng bié, lǒng tóu liú shuǐ, tì rén wū yè②。

王孙何许音尘绝，柔桑陌上吞声别。吞声别，陇头流水，替人呜咽②。

注释

①杜鹃啼血：白居易《琵琶行》中有“杜鹃啼血猿哀鸣”句，此处以杜鹃啼血，梨花飘雪比喻春色将暮时女主人公凄惨的心境。

②“王孙”二句：原来是女子心中爱慕的贵公子与她分别后没了音讯，当她回忆起在桑枝柔拂的陇头陌上忍泪吞声而别的情景时，心里更为凄惨。

Bamboo and Insects by Zhao Chang, Northern Song, hanging scroll, color on silk, 99.4 x 54.2 cm, kept in the National Museum of Tokyo, Japan. The painter drew meticulously the bamboo leaves and a variety of insects including butterfly, dragonfly, locust and long-horned beetle. Imitating Xu Chongsi's technique, he used rich colors to directly paint the melons and fruits on the bottom right corner without first making sketches.

◎ 竹虫图，赵昌，立轴，绢本设色，99.4×54.2cm，日本东京国立博物馆藏。此图画幽篁疏影，双钩填彩，以色之浓淡来显叶之向背、竿之盘曲。枝叶饱满，姿态多样。另有花卉野瓜、蝴蝶蜻蜓萦绕而飞，又绘天牛、螽斯，无不刻画入微，瓜叶果实又仿效徐崇嗣的"没骨"画法。设色浓丽而又不隐墨骨。

注 释

①凌波：形容女子轻盈的步履。语出曹植《洛神赋》"凌波微步，罗袜生尘。"横塘：苏州地名。《中吴纪闻》"（铸）有小筑在盘门之南十余里，地名横塘。"

②芳尘：美人身后的尘土。这里借指美人的身影。

③锦瑟华年：美好的年华。语出李商隐《无题》"锦色无端五十弦，一弦一柱思华年。"谁与度：即"与谁度"之倒装。

④月桥花院：小桥映月，春花满院。

⑤琐窗：有雕花格子的窗户。

⑥冉冉：缓缓流动。蘅皋：长着香草的水边高地。蘅：杜衡，香草名。

⑦彩笔：文彩华丽的词笔。传说齐梁时的作家江淹因得到了一支五色笔，写诗多美句。后来梦见郭璞向他讨还了这支笔，于是文思大不如前，当时人说是"江郎才尽"。事见《南史·江淹传》。

⑧闲愁：风情，男女爱恋之情。都：共。

TUNE: GREEN JADE CUP

— He Zhu

Never again will she tread on the lakeside lane. I follow with my eyes the fragrant dusts that rise. With whom is she now spending her delightful hours, playing on zither string, on a crescent-shaped bridge, in a yard full of flowers, or in a vermeil bower only known to spring?

At dusk the floating cloud leaves the grass-fragrant plain; with blooming brush I write heart-broken verse again. If you ask me how deep and wide I am lovesick, just see a misty plain where grass grows thick, a townful of willow down wafting on the breeze, or drizzling rain yellowing all mume-trees!

青玉案
— 贺铸

凌波不过横塘路①，但目送，芳尘去②。锦瑟华年谁与度③？月桥花院④，琐窗朱户⑤，只有春知处。

飞云冉冉蘅皋暮⑥，彩笔新题断肠句⑦。试问闲愁都几许⑧？一川烟草，满城风絮，梅子黄时雨。

Snow in Winter Woods, ascribed to Fan Kuan, Northern Song, hanging scroll, ink and wash on silk, 193.5 x 160.3 cm, kept in Tianjin Art Museum. Although it's ascribed to Fan, there has been much disagreement among scholars over its authentic authorship. The picture depicts the beautiful and magnificent scenery of snow-capped mountains in north China. The author used ink and wash to portray an undulating chain of mountains blanketed with snow and the bare trees on mountain tops. In terms of its drawing technique, it perfectly fits Fan's style.

◎ 雪景寒林图轴，北宋，范宽，绢本水墨，193.5×160.3cm，天津艺术博物馆藏。此图虽有范宽款识，但是否为其所作，历来颇有争议。此画描写了北方壮美的雪山景色。画家以水墨绘群山积雪，山顶枯树寒柯，山石高峻，雄气敦厚，有冒雪出云之势、凛凛寒气之感。抛开作者是谁不谈，单就绘画风格来看，确实是有范宽画风的巨作。

TUNE: SOVEREIGN OF WINE

— Zhou Bangyan

A row of willows shades the riverside. Their long, long swaying twigs have dyed the mist in green. How many times has the ancient Dyke seen the lovers part while wafting willowdown and drooping twigs caress the stream along the town! I come and climb up high to gaze on my homeland with longing eye. Oh, who could understand why should a weary traveller here stand? Along the shady way, from year to year, from day to day, how many branches have been broken to keep memories awoken?

Where are the traces of my bygone days? Again I drink to doleful lays in parting feast by lantern light, when pear blossoms announce the season clear and bright. Oh, slow down, wind speeding my boat like arrow-head; pole of bamboo half immersed in warm stream! Oh, post on post is left behind when I turn my head. My love is lost, still gazing as if lost in a dream.

How sad and drear! The farther I'm away, the heavier on my mind my grief will weigh. Gradually winds the river clear; deserted is pier on pier. The setting sun sheds here and there its parting ray. I will remember long the moonlit bower visited hand in hand with you, and the flute's plaintive song heard on the bridge bespangled with dew. Lost in the past now like a dream, my tears fall silently in stream.

Traveling Amid Streams and Mountains by Fan Kuan, Northern Song, hanging scroll, ink on silk, 206.3 x 103.3 cm, kept in the Palace Museum of Taipei. This is a picture of great power made with ingenious technique. Towering mountains make up nearly two-thirds of the picture's space. A waterfall rushes down the mountainside into a large pool hidden in a mist. In the foreground winds a stream in lush green trees, making viewers feel as if they are present on the scene.

◎ 溪山行旅图轴，北宋，范宽，绢本墨笔，206.3×103.3cm，台北故宫博物院藏。此图气势磅礴，章法奇特。雄厚而突兀的山头迎面矗立，占去了画面三分之二。山间瀑布，一落千丈。山下则被烟云拦腰遮断，空山一片，衬托出近景树木的欣容，流水之旋荡。浑厚壮阔的关中景色，如逼眼前，给人极强的视觉冲击力。

兰陵王 lán líng wáng

—— 周邦彦 zhōu bāng yàn

柳阴直①，烟里丝丝弄碧。隋堤上②，曾见几番，拂水飘绵送行色③！登临望故国④，谁识京华倦客？长亭路，年去岁来，应折柔条过千尺。

闲寻旧踪迹，又酒趁哀弦⑤，灯照离席。梨花榆火催寒食⑥。愁一箭风快⑦，半篙波暖，回头迢递便数驿⑧。望人在天北。

凄恻，恨堆积。渐别浦萦回，津堠岑寂⑨。斜阳冉冉春无极。念月榭携手⑩，露桥闻笛。沉思前事，似梦里，泪暗滴。

注 释

①柳阴直：堤柳的阴影连成一条整齐的直线。

②隋堤：指隋炀帝（604—618在位）时导汴水入运河所修的堤岸。

③飘绵：柳絮飘扬。

④故国：指故乡。

⑤哀弦：弦声轻柔，管声嘹亮，谓之豪竹哀丝。

⑥榆火：古俗以清明前一天（一说清明前两天）为寒食节。朝廷取榆柳新火以赐百官。民间也有"改火"的风俗。

⑦一箭风快：顺风驶帆，船快如箭。

⑧迢递：遥远。

⑨津堠：渡口曰津，哨所曰堠。

⑩月榭：月光映照的楼台。

Ripe Fruits Attracting a Bird by Lin Chun, Southern Song, album leaf, color on silk, 26.5 x 27 cm, kept in the Palace Museum of Beijing. A lively bird is twittering on a branch that bears rich fruits. The painting, though with a simple composition, is full of wit and interest.

◎ 果熟来禽图，林椿，册页，绢本设色，26.5 × 27cm，北京故宫博物院藏。此图绘有林檎果一枝，树上硕果丰熟，有一只小鸟立于枝上，翘起尾巴，挺起毛茸茸的胸脯，作欲飞的情态，形象生动可爱。叶与枝柯，仿佛随着鸟儿的动作在轻轻地颤动。果叶正反两面的枯荣之态刻画细致，虫蚀痕迹清晰。画面虽简单，却充满生机盎然的意趣，具有较强烈的感情色彩。

TUNE: BUDDHIST DANCERS

— Zhou Bangyan

The Milky-Way-like river winds from bend to bend, cranes fly over pure green waves with which wild ducks blend. Where is the returning boat of my dear one? From riverside tower I see but the setting sun.

Jealous of trees with mume blossoms aglow, heaven covers their branches with snow. If he uprolls the curtain in his bower, he'd pity the cold riverside flower.

注 释

①银河：此非天上银河，乃人间银河，以形容长江。
②此句指江上洲渚的各种飞鸟翻飞，漂浮于江上，万里长江波涛澄碧。
③梅浪：春天里梅树生长，枝叶繁盛，故称。

pú sà mán
菩萨蛮

zhōu bāng yàn
——周邦彦

yín hé wǎn zhuǎn sān qiān qǔ①, yù
银河 宛 转 三 千 曲①，浴
fú fēi lù chéng bō lù②, hé chù shì guī
凫 飞 鹭 澄 波 绿②。 何 处 是 归
zhōu xī yáng jiāng shàng lóu
舟 ？ 夕 阳 江 上 楼 。

tiān zēng méi làng fā③, gù xià fēng
天 憎 梅 浪 发③， 故 下 封
zhī xuě shēn yuàn juǎn lián kàn yīng lián jiāng
枝 雪 。 深 院 卷 帘 看 ， 应 怜 江
shàng hán
上 寒 。

92

Solitary Temple Among Snowy Hills by Fan Kuan, Northern Song, Hanging scroll, color on silk, 182.4 x 108.2cm, kept in the Palace Museum of Taipei. It's composed of two vertical scrolls. An ancient temple is faintly discernible among snowy mountains. The picture presents a chilly winter scene.

◎ 雪山萧寺图轴，北宋，范宽，绢本设色，182.4×108.2cm，台北故宫博物院藏。此图为双拼立轴。群峰矗立，气势险峻。山腰谷口之间，古寺萧条，半隐半现。旅人穿行于云关古栈雪岭之间。山腰山脚遍作密林，奇石上大树根柯槎枒，充满"树老风霜劲"之感。山石表面密点攒簇，表现了其"抢笔"技法的特点。

精选 宋词 与 宋画

TUNE: CRANE SOARING INTO THE SKY
WRITTEN IN THE LONG LIFE VILLAGE
— Zhou Bangyan

Long rain clears off when blows soft summer breeze, cicadas trill pellmell atop tall willow trees. From my bower the garden pool's far away; new lotus leaves stir when fish play.

Bed curtain thin lets feather fan blow in fresh air to chill the mat and pillow from deep courtyard still. My feeling as the weather nice brings me to earthly paradise.

hè chōng tiān
鹤 冲 天

lì shuǐ cháng shòu xiāng zuò
溧 水 长 寿 乡 作

zhōu bāng yàn
—— 周 邦 彦

méi yǔ jì ① shǔ fēng hé gāo liǔ luàn
梅 雨 霁 ，暑 风 和 ，高 柳 乱

chán duō xiǎo yuán tái xiè yuǎn chí bō yú xì
蝉 多 。 小 园 台 榭 远 池 波 ，鱼 戏

dòng xīn hé
动 新 荷 。

bó shā chú qīng yǔ shàn zhěn lěng diàn
薄 纱 厨 ，轻 羽 扇 ，枕 冷 簟

liáng shēn yuàn ② cǐ shí qíng xù cǐ shí tiān
凉 深 院 。 此 时 情 绪 此 时 天 ，

wú shì xiǎo shén xiān ③
无 事 小 神 仙 。

注 释

①霁：放晴。

②簟：竹制的席。

③"无事"句：浮生难得半日闲，特别是凄清连绵的梅雨终于停止后，夏风习习，高柳蝉鸣的时刻，小园香树，水远波平，鱼儿嬉游于莲叶间。薄薄的绿纱窗下，轻摇羽扇，躺在凉凉的竹席竹枕上。此情此景，还会有人不觉得自己活着赛过神仙吗？

94

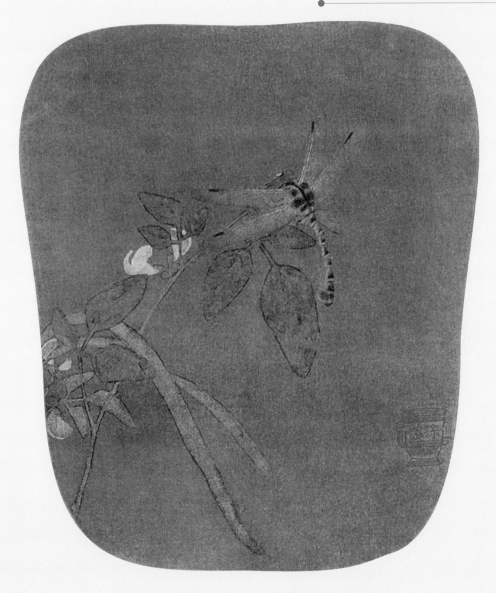

Pea Flowers and a Dragonfly, author unknown (formerly ascribedto Xu Xi), Southern Song, elliptic fan shaped, color on silk, 27 x 23 cm, kept in the Palace Museum of Beijing. The unknown artist made a meticulous depiction of the dragonfly while dashing off the pea flowers with just a few strokes. With all objects being well spaced, it's full of idyllic appeal.

◎ 豆花蜻蜓图页，南宋，无款，绢本设色，27×23cm，北京故宫博物院藏。此图旧传为徐熙所作。画面为长圆扇形，绘豆花上栖息一只黄褐色蜻蜓，枝叶微向下垂。整幅作品结构自然，疏密得当，色彩丰富，工写结合。其中蜻蜓的描绘尤为神妙，形态、纹络都刻画得细致入微。而豆花则以简笔写出，野趣天然。

TUNE: RIVERSIDE TOWN

— Xie Yi

The streamer flies among apricots in the breeze; brimming water wide spread, fallen petals dye the shore red. A boat athwart the ferry, the willow trees cast shadows deep green. I gaze southward on far-flung mountains high, my love cannot be seen, but grass spreads to the sky.

At sunset the mist veiled her bower, her rosy face sweet like a flower, with eyebrows penciled like a hill. I remember still that year before the painted screen we met with smiles. But now over the mountain pass tonight, severed for miles and miles, we share only the same moonlight.

注 释

①此用杜牧"借问酒家何处有,牧童遥指杏花村"句意。

②此用韦应物"野渡无人舟自横"句意。

③粉香融:指女人暖融融的脂粉气。淡眉峰:指她淡扫的蛾眉。

④"今夜月"三句化用南朝宋谢庄《月赋》中"美人迈今音尘阙,隔千里今共明月"之句。

jiāng chéng zǐ
江 城 子

—— xiè yì 谢逸

xìng huā cūn guǎn jiǔ qí fēng ①　shuǐ róng
杏 花 村 馆 酒 旗 风 ，水 溶

róng　yáng cán hóng　yě dù zhōu héng ②　yáng liǔ
溶 ， 扬 残 红 。 野 渡 舟 横 ， 杨 柳

lǜ yīn nóng　mèng duàn jiāng nán shān sè yuǎn　rén
绿 阴 浓 。 梦 断 江 南 山 色 远 ， 人

bū jiàn　cǎo lián kōng
不 见 ， 草 连 空 。

xī yáng lōu wài wǎn yān lōng　fěn xiāng
夕 阳 楼 外 晚 烟 笼 ， 粉 香

róng　dàn méi fēng ③　jì dé nián shí　xiāng jiàn
融 ， 淡 眉 峰 。 记 得 年 时 ， 相 见

huà píng zhōng　zhǐ yǒu guān shān jīn yè yuè　qiān
画 屏 中 。 只 有 关 山 今 夜 月 ， 千

lǐ wài　sù guāng tóng ④
里 外 ， 素 光 同 。

Flowering Peach, author unknown, Southern Song, round fan, color on silk, 24.8 x 27 cm, kept in the Palace Museum of Beijing. The unknown artist first sketched the contours of the peach blossoms, and then repeatedly used sweeping washes of wet ink to present rich color gradations, lending an implicit charm to the painting.

◎ 碧桃图，佚名，团扇，绢本设色，24.8 × 27cm，北京故宫博物院藏。此图绘碧桃两只，枝上的碧桃花有的吐露盛开，有的含苞欲放，风姿虽各异却无不饱含春意。全图画工极为精丽，花瓣用笔精严谨细，并于勾描后多层晕染，使桃花在淡雅中富有层次变化且不失主次疏密之分。故画面虽小，却意趣无穷，堪为南宋写生妙品。

TUNE: SEPARATION REGRETTED

— Mao Pang

Her face criss-crossed with tears, a flower bathed in dew; her saddened eyebrows knit like distant peaks in view. How can I not share her grief acute? What can we do but gaze at each other mute?

My broken cloud won't bring showers for thirsting flowers, lonely in morning and in evening hours. Tonight in mountains deep I'd ask the rising tide to bring my yearning heart to her at the seaside.

注　释

①此用白居易《长恨歌》"梨花一枝春带雨"句意。此词写毛滂与恋人的一段未了情。

②此用张泌《思越人》"黛眉愁聚着翠"词意。

③"此恨"句：离愁别恨对于双方是一样的折磨。

④"相觑"句：相视无言空自相对。觑，看。

⑤"断云"二句：离人的心境是落寞的，词人兼用宋玉《高唐赋》"旦为朝云，暮为行雨，朝朝暮暮，阳台之下"句意，喻这段行将结束的恋情。

⑥"今夜"二句：夜深山静，吩咐断魂与江潮一同归去，意极缠绵悱恻。

xī fēn fēi
惜　分　飞

—— māopáng
毛滂

lèi shī lán gān huā zhuó lù　　　　chóu dào
泪 湿 阑 干 花 着 露①， 愁 到
méi fēng bì jù　　cǐ hèn píng fēn qǔ　　gèng
眉 峰 碧 聚②。 此 恨 平 分 取③， 更
wú yán yǔ kōng xiāng qù
无 言 语 空 相 觑④。

duàn yún cán yǔ wú yì xù　　jì mò zhāo
断 云 残 雨 无 意 绪， 寂 寞 朝
zhāo mù mù　　jīn yè shān shēn chù　　duàn hún
朝 暮 暮⑤。 今 夜 山 深 处， 断 魂
fēn fù cháo huí qù
分 付 潮 回 去⑥。

Children Playing in Dragon Boat Festival (partial) by Su Zhuo, Southern Song, color on silk, kept in the Palace Museum of Taipei. The artist vividly portrayed three kids in *dudou* (diamond-shaped cloth worn by a child over the chest and abdomen and attached by a loop round the neck and strings fastened behind the back). In the painting a kid holds a toad to scare his pal while a third one is trying to rescue the frightened.

◎ 端阳婴戏（局部），南宋，苏焯，绢本设色，台北故宫博物院藏。画面上三名稚龄儿童皆穿肚兜，露出胖润的双臂，居高的一位手拎一只蟾蜍，逗吓另一名儿童，被吓的小孩则双手护头，表现出惊恐状，还有一名儿童则来解围。画家透过线条，将人物刻画得神气活现。

精选

宋词与宋画

TUNE: BUDDHIST DANCERS

WRITTEN IN THE BOAT FOR A FRIEND

— Su Xiang

Before my eyes mist-veiled trees on mist-veiled trees stand; evening clouds shed rain drop by drop on lotus blooms. Gulls float along smoke-darkened sand; in overbrimming green rushes autumn looms.

I've gone overseas but stay by pools and woods. My homeless grief won't cease; the wind slants our white hoods.

注　释

①"鸥泛"二句：鸥鸟泛游沙洲，在树枝停栖。绿色的菰蒲秋天时长满了平川。

②"未成"二句：宦游四海的志向未能实现，姑且先做这里林塘的主人吧。

③"客恨"二句：离开家乡的人恼恨渡口深沉开阔，白叠巾也被风吹得歪斜了。

pú sà mán
菩萨蛮

zhōu yàn dá zhōu zhōng zuò
周彦达舟中作

sū xiāng
—— 苏庠

yǎn zhōng dié dié yān zhōng shù   wǎn yún
眼 中 叠 叠 烟 中 树 ， 晚 云

diǎn diǎn fān hé yǔ   ōu fàn zhǔ biān yān
点 点 翻 荷 雨 。 鸥 泛 渚 边 烟 ，

lǜ pú qiū mǎn chuān ①
绿 蒲 秋 满 川 。

wèi chéng jiāng hǎi qù   liáo zuò lín táng
未 成 江 海 去 ， 聊 作 林 塘

zhǔ ②   kè hèn kuò wú jīn   fēng xié bái dié
主 。 客 恨 阔 无 津 ， 风 斜 白 叠

jīn ③
巾 。

Shaking Jujubes off the Tree (partial), author unknown, color on silk, 138.6 x 101.6 cm, kept in the Palace Museum of Taipei. In the painting some children shake ripe jujubes off a tree while some others are picking up those falling on ground.

◎ 扑枣图（局部），无款，绢本设色，138.6 × 101.6cm，台北故宫博物院藏。画面描写秋天，枣树上的枣熟了，七个小孩有的在扑打树上的枣儿，一时间枣落满地，有的正在地上双手并用拣枣的情景，充满生活情趣。

精选
宋词
与
宋画

TUNE: SILK-WASHING STREAM
INKY MUME BLOSSOMS
— Hui Hong

At dusk a boat is floating on the river wide.

Whose hermitage stands lonely by the riverside? A

branch of mume at leisure stretches o'er the wall.

The mume veiled in moonlight sends fragrance

on the wing; it longs for home, but only stays for

coming spring. The wind-stirred petals show their

sorrow one and all.

注 释

①"日暮"二句：描写的是日暮时分，靠近江流空阔苍茫的沧洲的庭院。

②"一枝"句：一枝梅花闲闲地无意露出墙头。

③"数朵"二句：这枝条上的数朵幽香和着月色更显幽暗，暮春十分独自为春而逗留。

④"风撩"句：风吹过，撩起片片落花，引人伤春的闲愁斋绪。

huàn xī shā
浣溪沙
miǎo gāo mò méi
妙高墨梅

huì hóng
—— 惠洪

rì mù jiāng kōng chuán zì liú   shuí jiā
日 暮 江 空 船 自 流 ， 谁 家
yuàn luò jìn cāng zhōu   yì zhī xián xiá chū qiáng
院 落 近 沧 洲① ？ 一 枝 闲 暇 出 墙
tóu
头②。

shù duǒ yōu xiāng huò yuè àn   shí fēn
数 朵 幽 香 和 月 暗 ， 十 分
guī yì wèi chūn liú   fēng liáo piàn piàn shì
归 意 为 春 留③。 风 撩 片 片 是
xiān chóu
闲 愁④。

Bird on a Snowy Tree Bough by Li Di, Southern Song, hanging scroll, color on silk, 116.1 x 53 cm, kept in Shanghai Museum. A shrike perches in a thorny tree covered by light snow. It's a masterpiece of the painter in his old age. The bird was drawn in gaudy colors directly without first making sketches.

◎ 雪树寒禽图，李迪，绢本设色，116.1 × 53cm，上海博物馆藏。此图写竹叶覆雪，轻染薄雪的棘树上，栖息着一只伯劳。山坡以粗笔勾出，写一丛衰草，更添雪意。双钩写竹、树干，敷色渲染。雀鸟以没骨及勾勒相结合绘出，写实生动。此画是画家晚年的精心之作。

TUNE: SONG OF DIVINATION
ENJOYING THE BREEZE IN PHOENIX PAVILION ON THE NIGHT OF THE 5TH DAY OF THE 8TH MOON

— Ye Mengde

The crescent moon hangs on tree-tips; in dried pool hidden water drips. On painted eaves I see now and then sparse stars fall, here and there a few dots of fireflies small.

I'm not much sick for native hill, but homesickness haunts me still. I'll write new songs for gatherers of lotus seed, but find on boundless water mist-veiled reed.

注 释

① "新月" 二句：作者坐于亭上，四周寂静，抬眼望见新月挂在林梢，耳畔有水声汩汩流出于将要枯竭的水沼。

② "时见" 二句：又不时地见到几颗稀疏的晚星渐渐消逝于画檐的一角，这时有几点萤火在眼前乱舞起来。

③ "归意" 二句：作者刚刚出来纳凉还不想回去，所以就周围四处走走，未曾想着走着又回到了原来的地方。

④ "欲寄" 二句：想要寄托些心意于采菱船，却不料它不知何时已远远驶去，只留下作者有些失意地怅望着一片烟波浩荡的阔大水面。

bǔ suàn zǐ
卜 算 子

bā yuè wǔ rì yè fēng huáng tíng nà liáng
八 月 五 日 夜 凤 凰 亭 纳 凉

yè mèng dé
—— 叶 梦 得

xīn yuè guà lín shāo ān shuǐ míng kū
新 月 挂 林 梢 ， 暗 水 鸣 枯

zhāo ① shí jiàn shū xīng luò huà yán jǐ diǎn
沼 。 时 见 疏 星 落 画 檐 ， 几 点

liú yíng xiǎo ②
流 萤 小 。

guī yì yǐ wú duō gù zuò lián huán
归 意 已 无 多 ， 故 作 连 环

rào ③ yù jì xīn shēng wèn cǎi líng shuǐ kuò
绕 。 欲 寄 新 声 问 采 菱 ， 水 阔

yān bō miǎo ④
烟 波 渺 。

Buffalo Boys (part one and two) by Yan Ciping, Southern Song, handscroll, color on silk, 35 x 90 cm each, kept in Nanjing Museum. Genre painting was all the rage during the Southern Song Dynasty, covering a wide range of subjects, which is seldom seen throughout the history of China's fine arts. Differing from the literati painting that tended to create an artistic ambience, in his famous *Buffalo Boys* Yan took great pains to depict the boys and their buffalo to the last detail.

◎ 牧牛图卷（之一、之二），南宋，阎次平，绢本设色，每幅 35 × 90cm，南京博物院藏。南宋时期反映广阔社会生活的风俗画十分活跃，题材也非常广泛，几乎涉及到生活的各个方面，这在中国美术史上是罕见的。阎次平的这件《牧牛图卷》，在传世的风俗画作品中素以表现牧童生活著称。图中景物描写自然，没有追求文人强调的意境，而是着力于牧童与水牛的神态刻画，十分生动。

TUNE: EVERLASTING LONGING

RAIN

— Moqi Yong

Watch after watch and drop by drop, the rain falls on banana leaves without stop. Within the window by the candlelight, for you I'm longing all night.

I cannot seek for dreams, nor banish sorrow. The rain cares not for what I dislike, it seems; on marble steps it drips until the morrow.

注　释

①上半阕写的是作者坐在灯窗下，听雨打芭蕉一声接一声，无奈时间也一更天又一更天地飞逝，只有作者心中怀想着，思念着，寄予无限情思于远方的爱人。

②下半阕写作者芭蕉雨夜辗转难眠，梦也做不成，心中爱越深恨亦越切，心绪起伏难平，他不觉责怪起芭蕉雨来了，忧愁的人不喜欢听这凄切的声音，于石阶上徒自滴到天明。

长 相 思
chāng xiāng sī

雨
yǔ

—— 万俟咏
mò qí yǒng

一 声 声， 一 更 更， 窗 外
yì shēng shēng， yì gēng gēng， chuāng wài

芭 蕉 窗 里 灯， 此 时 无 限 情 ①。
bā jiāo chuāng lǐ dēng， cǐ shí wú xiàn qíng

梦 难 成， 恨 难 平， 不 道
mèng nán chéng， hèn nán píng， bú dào

愁 人 不 喜 听， 空 阶 滴 到 明 ②。
chóu rén bù xǐ tīng， kōng jiē dī dào míng

Hunting Dog by Li Di, Southern Song, album leaf, color on silk, 26.5 x 26.9 cm, kept in the Palace Museum of Beijing. As an ancient saying goes, it's easier to draw a ghost than a dog or horse since the images of the latter are familiar to everybody. The portray depicting a dog hunting for a prey animal by scent is most vivid and truly lifelike.

◎ 猎犬图，李迪，绢本设色，26.5 × 26.9cm，北京故宫博物院藏。中国古代画论有云："画鬼魅易，图犬马难。"意指像狗、马之类，人们经常与之相处，对它们的习性特征都很熟悉，所以要把它们画得让人们认可并不是很容易的事。此图画一猎犬漫步前行，似乎正循着什么气味而行，神态专注而机敏，刻画精细入微，实可谓形神兼备。

TUNE: SHORTENED FORM OF MAGNOLIA FLOWER

— Zhu Dunru

Uninvited to wine, I spread a blanket and sit beneath a pine. Drinking, I write verse fine, mume blossoms serve as attendants divine.

Drunken in happy hours, when the bright moon flies down, I sleep beneath the flowers. I dance--Who knows my delight? My hood covered with blooms, my cup brimming with moonlight.

注 释

①"无人"二句：写作者悠然自得的心境，没人请我自己在松间铺上毡坐下。自娱自乐，令人艳羡。

②"酌酒"二句：饮酒吟诗，自斟自饮，更调弄梅花，以之作伴，此时梅花是我最好的侍儿。充分体现出作者怡然自得的心情。

③"心欢"二句：心中欢愉，饮得半醉，觉得明月也从天边飞来与我一道花中共眠。

④"醉舞"二句：醉中我舞影零乱，看见花朵仿佛绣满我轻纱的罗巾，月光满盛于我的酒杯。

jiǎn zì mù lán huā
减字木兰花

— zhū dūn rú
朱敦儒

wú rén qǐng wǒ   wǒ zì pū zhān sōng
无 人 请 我 ， 我 自 铺 毡 松

xià zuò ①   zhuó jiǔ cái shī   tiáo nòng méi huā
下 坐 。 酌 酒 裁 诗 ， 调 弄 梅 花

zuò shì ér ②
作 侍 儿 。

xīn huān yì zuì   míng yuè fēi lái huā
心 欢 易 醉 ， 明 月 飞 来 花

xià shuì ③   zuì wǔ shuí zhī   huā mǎn shā jīn
下 睡 。 醉 舞 谁 知 ？ 花 满 纱 巾

yuè mǎn bēi ④
月 满 杯 。

Green Oranges by Ma Lin, Southern Song, round fan, color on silk, 23 x 23.5 cm, kept in the Palace Museum of Beijing. In this sketch masterwork, the artist portrayed in a meticulous and realistic way an orange branch over-hung with fruits. A good crop is in prospect.

◎ 橘绿图，马麟，册页，绢本设色，23 × 23.5cm，北京故宫博物院藏。此图画橘梗几只，穿插错落，从右向左斜出。画面果繁叶茂，丰满多姿，一派丰收景象。尤其引人注目的是画家细致描绘出橘子全熟、半熟的不同状态，充分反映了画家高超的写实功力。图中枝叶、果实勾勒填彩，设色鲜丽，形神兼备，不愧为写生妙作。

TUNE: TREADING ON GRASS

— Zhou Zizhi

My thoughts waft like gossemer light; you'll go off as willow down flies. In vain we gaze at each other with tearful eyes. Thousands of willow twigs hang low by riverside, but none of them can stop your orchid boat on the tide.

Past setting sun wild geese in flight, on mist-veiled isle grass lost to sight, it looks like a boundless ocean of grief and sorrow. But now do not think of what I shall do tomorrow! Alas! How can I pass this endless lonely night.

踏莎行
tà suō xíng

—— 周紫芝
zhōu zǐ zhī

情似游丝，人如飞絮①，
qíng sì yóu sī rén rú fēi xù

泪珠阁定空相觑②。一溪烟柳
lèi zhū gé dìng kōng xiāng qù   yì xī yān liǔ

万丝垂，无因系得兰舟住③。
wàn sī chuí   wú yīn xì dé lán zhōu zhù

雁过斜阳，草迷烟渚④，
yàn guò xié yáng   cǎo mí yān zhǔ

如今已是愁无数。明朝且做
rú jīn yǐ shì chóu wú shù   míng zhāo qiě zuò

莫思量，如何过得今宵去！
mò sī liàng   rú hé guò dé jīn xiāo qù

注 释

①此二句用冯延巳"满眼游丝兼落絮"词意，将一句折为两句，分别道出了情人分离时的特定情境。

②"泪珠"句：两双满含泪水的眼睛，一动不动地彼此相视。"空"字将无限惆怅全部透露。

③此二句是说两岸杨柳垂下千千碧丝，却无法把那木兰舟留下。含人黯然魂消。

④烟渚：烟雾迷蒙的水中小洲。

110

Evening Snow and Winter Birds by Ma Lin, Southern Song, handscroll, color on silk, 27.6 x 42.9 cm, kept in the Palace Museum of Taipei. In a world of ice and snow, two birds cower in a withered tree drawn with powerful strokes. The painting creates a bleak winter scene.

◎ 暮雪寒禽图，马麟，绢本设色，27.6 × 42.9cm，中国台北故宫博物院藏。此图以清丽的笔法，绘出冰天雪地之中，山竹覆雪，两只寒禽躲在山石之下的枯枝上过夜的景象。以淡墨渲染全景，烘托出雪意，双钩写竹，用笔劲力。整幅画萧瑟冷峭，意境幽远。

TUNE: HILLSIDE PAVILION

— Zhao Ji

Petal on petal of well-cut fine silk ice-white, evenly touched with rouge light, your fashion new and overflowing charm make shy all fragrant palace maids on high. How easy 'tis for you to fade! You cannot bear the cruel wind and shower's raid. I'm sad to ask the courtyard sad and drear how many waning springs have haunted here?

My heart is overladen with deep grief. How could a pair of swallows give relief? Could they know what I say? 'Neath boundless sky my ancient palace's far away. Between us countless streams and mountains stand. Could swallows find my native land? Could I forget these mountains and these streams? But I cannot go back except in dreams. I know that dreams can never be believed, but now e'en dreams won't come to me!

Arhat by Liu Songnian, Southern Song, hanging scroll, color on silk, 117 x 55.8 cm, kept in the Palace Museum of Taipei. Imitating Li Tang's style, Liu was well versed in landscape and figure painting. In his works he often matched the characters and the natural setting perfectly. In this picture he created vivid and clear-cut images of an aged arhat and a young waiter. Even the depiction of old trees, monkeys and deer is so enchanting that viewers cannot tear themselves away from it.

◎罗汉图轴,南宋,刘松年,绢本设色,117 × 55.8cm,台北故宫博物院藏。刘松年工山水人物,山水画法受李唐影响,但变雄健为典雅,画风严谨不苟,水墨青绿兼擅,作品中山水与人物常占有同等地位。这件《罗汉图》中,对人物神态的刻画尤为精到,如对老年尊者目光神色的刻画,年幼侍者清秀形象的塑造等,皆生动感人,甚至对老树、猿猴、麋鹿的描绘,也都生动有致,耐人玩味。

燕山亭

—— 赵佶

裁剪冰绡，轻叠数重，淡着胭脂匀注①。新样靓妆，艳溢香融，羞杀蕊珠宫女②。易得凋零，更多少无情风雨③！愁苦，问院落凄凉，几番春暮④？

凭寄离恨重重⑤，这双燕何曾会人言语⑥！天遥地远，万水千山，知他故宫何处⑦？怎不思量，除梦里有时曾去⑧。无据，和梦也有时不做⑨。

注 释

①冰绡：白色的丝织品。匀注：均匀地点染。以上三句描写杏花的鲜艳。前两句写花瓣，后一句写花的颜色。赵佶即宋徽宗。

②靓妆：美丽的妆饰。艳溢：光彩四射。香融：香气散发。蕊珠宫女：指仙女。

③更：更加。

④院落：庭院。

⑤凭寄：这里有烦请传寄的意思。

⑥会：理解。

⑦故宫：作者往昔所居住的皇宫。

⑧思量：想念。除：除非。

⑨无据：不可靠。和：连。

Auspicious Cranes by Zhao Ji (Emperor Huizong), Northern Song, handscroll, color on silk, 51 x 138.2 cm, kept in Liaoning Provincial Museum. Eighteen red-crowned cranes circle above the imposing Xuande Gate in Kaifeng, the Northern Song capital, while two others stand on the ridge of the palace. The painting shows an auspicious and peaceful atmosphere.

◎ 瑞鹤图，宋徽宗赵佶，绢本设色，51 × 138.2cm，辽宁博物馆藏。在这幅帛画中，徽宗描绘了发生于1112年的一件事，当时一群白鹤飞至一座宫殿，为纪念这一吉兆，他赋诗一首并作此画。此图画庄严耸立的汴梁宣德门，门上方彩云缭绕，十八只神态各异的丹顶鹤在上空翱翔盘旋，另两只站立在殿脊的鸱吻之上，回首相望，天空及宫殿周围的祥云皆以平涂渲染，更烘托出仙鹤动飞之势和曼妙体态，气氛祥和吉庆。

精选

宋词与宋画

TUNE: DREAMLIKE SONG

—Li Qi

At early dawn no jade-white beauty is in sight.
Long, long I sigh to clouds on high. Green water
brims over the rail-girt pool; beyong bamboos I
find mume branch with ease sway in the breeze.
How wonderful! How wonderful to see the beauty
steeped in moonlight at dead of night!

rú mèng lìng
如 梦 令

—— 李祁 lǐ qí

bú jiàn yù rén qīng xiǎo, cháng xiào yì
不 见 玉 人 清 晓 , 长 啸 一

shēng yún miǎo ① bì shuǐ mǎn lán táng, zhú wài
声 云 杪 ① 。 碧 水 满 阑 塘 , 竹 外

yì zhī fēng niǎo ② qí miào, qí miào, bàn
一 枝 风 袅 ② 。 奇 妙 , 奇 妙 , 半

yè shān kōng yuè jiǎo
夜 山 空 月 皎 。

注 释

① 此二句写诗人清晨起来不见佳人，于是长啸一声，声入云霄。

② 此二句写碧水溢满了波光粼粼的池塘，竹林外一阵风起。

Goddess of Luo (partial), author unknown, Northern Song, handscroll, color on silk, 51.2 x 1157 cm, kept in the Palace Museum of Beijing. Legend goes that when passing through the Luoshui River, Cao Zhi of the State of Wei during the Three Kingdoms composed a poem titled "The Goddess of Luo." Since then the oft-quoted poem has stimulated the creative inspiration of many later painters. In this scroll mountains and waters were drawn in ink and wash and light color, and figures and houses in rich colors. Interestingly, swimmers beside the berthed boat lend a secular flavor to it.

◎ 洛神赋图卷（局部），北宋，无款，绢本设色，51.2 × 1157cm，北京故宫博物院藏。三国曹魏时曹植路过洛水，创作了一篇脍炙人口的佳作《洛神赋》，从此之后，文中所描绘的那种天上与人间难以企及的爱情，便成为许多画家创作的灵感。这件作品即是依文而作。图中山水用水墨淡着色绘制，而人物、屋宇则施以重彩，有瑰丽的美感。有意思的是，泊船旁边水中的游泳者，为画面增添了一许风俗画的意味。

TUNE: A DREAMLIKE SONG

— Li Qingzhao

Last night the strong wind blew with a rain fine; sound sleep did not dispel the aftertaste of wine. I ask the maid rolling up the screen. "The same crab apple," says she, "can be seen." "But don't you know, oh, don't you know the red should languish and the green should grow?"

如梦令 (rú mèng lìng)

— 李清照 (lǐ qīng zhào)

昨夜雨疏风骤（zuó yè yǔ shū fēng zhòu），浓睡不消残酒（nóng shuì bù xiāo cán jiǔ）。试问卷帘人①（shì wèn juǎn lián rén），却道海棠依旧（què dào hǎi táng yī jiù）。知否？知否？（zhī fǒu? zhī fǒu?）应是绿肥红瘦②（yīng shì lǜ féi hóng shòu）。

注 释

①卷帘人：指侍女。

②绿肥红瘦：叶多花少，与绿暗红稀同义。

118

Cherry-apple Blossoms by Lin Chun, Southern Song, round fan, color on silk, 23.4 x 24 cm, kept in the Palace Museum of Taipei. Following the example of Zhao Chang, Lin drew flowers and birds with delicate touches as seen in this picture, representing the typical style of the imperial-court decorative painting.

◎ 海棠图，林椿，团扇，绢本设色，23.4 × 24cm，中国台北故宫博物院藏。林椿的花鸟师法赵昌，刻画精细，色彩淡雅，有生动之姿。此图海棠勾画、晕染，皆工整细致，栩栩如生，特别是海棠花以铅白、胭脂设色，在粉嫩晶莹中呈清丽端雅的气质，是南宋院体画的代表风格。

精选
宋词
与
宋画

TUNE: A TWIG OF MUME BLOSSOMS

— Li Qingzhao

Fragrant lotus blooms fade, autumn chills mat of jade. My silk robe doffed, I float alone in orchid boat. Who in the cloud would bring me letters in brocade? When swans come back in flight, my bower is steeped in moonlight.

As fallen flowers drift and water runs its way, one longing leaves no traces but overflows two places. O how can such lovesickness be driven away? From eyebrows kept apart, again it gnaws my heart.

一剪梅

— 李清照

红藕香残玉簟秋①，轻解罗裳，独上兰舟。云中谁寄锦书来②？雁字回时，月满西楼。

花自飘零水自流，一种相思，两处闲愁。此情无计可消除，才下眉头，又上心头③。

注　释

①红藕：红色的莲花。玉簟：莹润如玉的竹席。

②锦书：相思的书信。窦滔徒放流沙，其妻苏若兰织锦为回文诗以赠之。词情凄婉动人。事见《晋书·窦滔妻苏氏传》。

③以上三句说，眉头方才不皱了，心里却又想起来了。

120

渾如冷蝶宿花房
擁抱檀心憶舊香
開到寒梢尤可愛
此般必是漢宮粧

層叠冰綃

Layers on Layers of Icy Silk by Ma Lin, Southern Song, hanging scroll, color on silk, 101.5 x 49.6 cm, kept in the Palace Museum of Beijing. In this scroll the court painter drew two blossoming plum branches to go along with a poem inscribed by Emperor Ningzong's consort surnamed Yang, in which plum flowers were compared to the maids in the Han Dynasty imperial palace.

◎ 层叠冰绡图轴,南宋,马麟,绢本设色,101.5×49.6cm。此图画梅花两枝,疏枝绿萼。一枝昂首,一枝低头含笑,充分表达出梅花俏丽的姿容。笔法精工俏丽,故有"宫梅"之称。画幅中有宋宁宗皇后杨氏所提"层叠冰绡"四字,上部又题七言诗一首,把梅花喻为汉宫中的美女,使之更增添了感情色彩。

TUNE: SLOW SLOW SONG

— Li Qingzhao

I look for what I miss, I know not what it is. I feel so sad, so drear, so lonely, without cheer. How hard is it to keep me fit in this lingering cold! Hardly warmed up by cup on cup of wine so dry, oh, how can I endure the drift of evening wind so swift? It breaks my heart, alas! to see the wild geese pass for they are my acquaintances of old.

The ground is covered with yellow flowers, faded and fallen in showers. Who will pick them up now? Sitting alone at the window, how could I but quicken the pace of darkness that won't thicken? On the plane leaves a fine rain drizzles as twilight grizzles. Oh, what can I do with a grief beyond belief!

White Roses by Ma Yuan, Southern Song, album leaf, color on silk, 26.2 x 25.8 cm, kept in the Palace Museum of Beijing. The artist outlined the petals with fine lines, and then filled in with running ink. It has a refined, exquisite flavor.

◎ 白蔷薇图页，南宋，马远，绢本设色，26.2 × 25.8cm，北京故宫博物院藏。此图绘一枝轻灵润秀，生机勃发的折枝白蔷薇，用细笔勾花瓣而白粉晕染，花叶用线勾描而染一汁绿。枝干苍劲而润挺。全图用笔严谨，一丝不苟，画风清丽。设色淡雅，气韵生动。

声声慢

—— 李清照

寻寻觅觅，冷冷清清，凄凄惨惨戚戚①。乍暖还寒时候，最难将息②。三杯两盏淡酒，怎敌他晚来风急？雁过也，正伤心，却是旧时相识③。

满地黄花堆积，憔悴损，而今有谁堪摘④！守着窗儿，独自怎生得黑⑤？梧桐更兼细雨，到黄昏点点滴滴。这次第，怎一个愁字了得⑥！

注 释

①戚戚：愁苦之貌。

②将息：调养休息。

③旧时相识：意谓南飞的鸿雁却是曾为她捎过书信的老相识。可如今却再不能给她带来慰籍了。这是一种想象之词。

④黄花：指菊花。谁：何，什么。

⑤怎生：怎样。生，语助词。

⑥次第：光景、情况。

Mynah by Fa-chang, Southern Song, hanging scroll, ink and wash on paper, 78.5 x 39 cm, kept in the National Museum of Tokyo, Japan. Fa-chang, a monk painter, portrayed a mynah standing on the trunk of a pine tree in an unconventional style. He used rich ink to draw the bird with just a few strokes, and sketched part of the trunk and several pine needles here and there with light ink to indicate the tree's greatness. A vine winding round the trunk lends a delightful taste to the painting.

◎ 叭叭鸟图，法常，立轴，纸本水墨，78.5×39cm，日本东京国立美术馆藏。法常是南宋僧人，所作图画笔墨简洁严整，粗中带细，疏放随意又不失稳重。此图画八哥鸟立于老松干上，鸟身以极为概括的淡墨和浓墨画出，用笔与用墨十分简练，但鸟俯首啄羽的动态却生动自然。松干和松枝以淡墨写出，又绕以富有变化的藤枝，虚实相映，笔简墨润，堪称逸品的典范之作。

TUNE: GATHERING MULBERRIES

— Lu Benzhong

I'm grieved to find you unlike the moon at its best, north, south, east, west. North, south, east, west, it would accompany me without any rest.

I am grieved to find you like the moon which would fain now wax, now wane. You wax and wane. When will you come around like the full moon again?

采桑子
cǎi sāng zǐ

——吕本中

恨君不似江楼月①，南北东西。南北东西，只有相随无别离。

恨君却似江楼月，暂满还亏。暂满还亏②，待得团圆是几时③？

注 释

①江楼：江边的楼阁。

②暂满还亏：暂时圆满了一下，却又亏缺不圆了。

③团圆：《乐府雅词》作"团团"。

Canary on a Pomegranate Branch, author unknown, Southern Song, album leaf, color on silk, 24.6 x 25.4 cm, kept in the Palace Museum of Beijing. A canary holding a worm in the beak stands on a branch hung with heavy pomegranates. It's painted in bright and strikingly contrasting colors.

◎ 榴枝黄鸟图页，南宋，无款，绢本设色，24.6 × 25.4cm，北京故宫博物院藏。此图绘黄鸟一只，嘴啄小虫，栖于榴枝上，神形毕肖。图中枝梗从左向斜出，沉甸甸的石榴挂于枝干。榴叶萧瑟，鸟的羽毛用淡黄色染后，再用粉白以短而细的笔触勾描，具有毛茸茸的质感。鸟的翅膀和尾部等处，浓淡墨色参用，设色鲜艳而又对比鲜明。

TUNE: THE PRINCE RECALLED
SONG OF SPRING
— Li Chongyuan

Luxuriant grass reminds me of my roving mate.
In vain my heart breaks in willow-shaded tower high.
"Better go home!" How could I bear the cuckoo's
cry! The evening is growing late, the rain beats on
pear blossoms, I shut up the gate.

注　释

①此句从《楚词·招隐士》"王孙游兮不归,春草生兮萋萋"化出。王孙:公子哥儿。

②杜宇:杜鹃。鸣声凄绝,音似"不如归去"。

③此句从"梨花满地不开门"化出。

yì wǎng sūn
忆 王 孙

chūn cí
春 词

lǐ chóng yuán
—— 李 重 元

qī qī fāng cǎo yì wǎng sūn ① liǔ
萋 萋 芳 草 忆 王 孙 ， 柳
wài gāo lóu kōng duàn hún dù yǔ shēng shēng bù
外 高 楼 空 断 魂 。 杜 宇 声 声 不
rěn wén ② yù huáng hūn yǔ dǎ lí huā shēn
忍 闻 。 欲 黄 昏 ， 雨 打 梨 花 深
bì mén ③
闭 门 。

Caiwei (Picking Thornferns) by Li Tang, Southern Song, handscroll, light color on silk, 27.2 x 90.5 cm, kept in the Palace Museum of Beijing. This picture draws materials from the story of Bo Yi and Shu Qi, two scions of the Shang imperial family. After King Wu of Zhou toppled the Shang Dynasty, both Bo Yi and Shu Qi ran off and became hermits, living on wild herbs in the Shouyang Mountain in today's Henan Province. Li gave a vivid depiction of the two characters.

◎ 采薇图，南宋，李唐，绢本淡设色，27.2×90.5cm，北京故宫博物院藏。这幅画取材于西周（前1046-前771）王朝的建立者周武王伐纣时伯夷和叔齐的故事。伯夷和叔齐是商朝（前1600-前1046）的皇族，是殷商诸侯孤竹君的两个儿子。他们认为周武王伐纣是臣子叛逆，所以对周武王讨伐纣王曾拦道相谏，商亡以后，他们不食周粟，不做周臣，隐居在河南省的首阳山上，以采薇菜活命。宋人画这种题材的画，都是感于时事，用以自励，李唐的《采薇图》是这类画作中的突出之作，对叔齐和伯夷两人的神态表现得尤其生动。

TUNE: EVERLASTING LONGING

— Deng Su

The hills near by and mountains high extend with misty water as far as the sky; the longing maple leaves turn to red dye.

Chrysanthemums sigh; chrysanthemums die. You don't come back when wild geese westward fly, a screen of breeze and moonlight left before my eye.

cháng xiāng sī lìng
长 相 思 令

—— dèng sù
邓 肃

yì chóng shān， liǎng chóng shān， shān yuǎn
一 重 山， 两 重 山， 山 远

tiān gāo yān shuǐ hán。 xiāng sī fēng yè dān ①。
天 高 烟 水 寒。 相 思 枫 叶 丹 ①。

jú huā kāi， jú huā cán， yàn yǐ
菊 花 开， 菊 花 残， 雁 已

xī fēi rén wèi huán， yì lián fēng yuè xián ②。
西 飞 人 未 还， 一 帘 风 月 闲 ②。

注 释

①此句形容相思之深，从春至秋，一直到思念得枫叶红透为止。

②此句指思念远人，因孤独，总觉一帘风月悠悠，寂寞难耐。

130

Four Goats by Chen Juzhong, Southern Song, album leaf, light color on silk, 22.5 x 24 cm, kept in the Palace Museum of Beijing. Three goats fight with each other, while the other one looks down from a height, making no move. The artist applied light ink to set off the slope. It's a very dynamic painting.

◎ 四羊图页，南宋，陈居中，绢本淡设色，22.5 × 24cm，北京故宫博物院藏。此图绘四只山羊在枯树下打斗、观望的不同动态，形象生动，逗人喜爱。全图用笔简练朴实，色调柔和中又有对比。以大面积淡墨渲染出坡地，将天地区分开来，并很好地衬托了画面的主体。图中景物高低错落，画面富于变化。

TUNE: THE RIVER ALL RED

— Yue Fei

Wrath sets on end my hair, I lean on railings where I see the drizzling rain has ceased. Raising my eyes towards the skies, I heave long sighs, my wrath not yet appeased. To dust is gone the fame achieved in thirty years; like cloud-veiled moon the thousand-mile land disappears. Should youthful heads in vain turn grey, we would regret for aye.

Lost our capitals, what a burning shame! How can we generals quench our vengeful flame! Driving our chariots of war, we'd go to break through our relentless foe. Valiantly we'd cut off each head; laughing, we'd drink the blood they shed. When we've reconquered our lost land, in triumph would return our army grand.

Plum and Peacocks, Song Dynasty, album leaf, color on silk, 24.3 x 31.6 cm, kept in the Palace Museum of Beijing. The author was surnamed Ma, but his given name remains unknown. A plum tree and a green cypress are separated by sparse bamboos and wild flowers. A male peacock stands on the trunk of the cypress, while the female one hunts for food leisurely on the ground. The painting is overflowing with wit.

◎ 红梅孔雀图，册页，绢本设色，24.3 × 31.6cm，北京故宫博物院藏。此图作者姓马，但名字已不可考。图中一棵苍郁的翠柏和一株老干纵横的红梅，间之以疏竹野卉，花叶交参中，一只雄孔雀立于柏树上，羽毛丰美，雌孔雀在树下觅食，步态轻盈。画面富丽堂皇之中又有一种清雅淡泊的意味，虽接近"黄家富贵"体制，但用笔却较之疏散通脱，有意趣横生之妙。

133

注 释

①怒发冲冠：愤怒已极，竖起的头发把帽子都冲掉了。这是夸张的说法。语出《史记·廉颇蔺相如列传》："相如因持璧却立倚柱，怒发上冲冠。"

②抬望眼：抬头遥望。

③三十功名尘与土：意谓半生功业声名不过在车尘马足间奔走而已。

④八千里路云和月：意指南征北战的漫漫长途都是在风云星月中驰驱度过的。

⑤等闲：随便，轻易。

⑥靖康耻：指宋钦宗靖康二年(1127)金兵攻陷汴京掳走徽、钦二帝的政治惨变。

⑦贺兰山：亦名阿拉善山，在宁夏阿拉善旗东界，当时是西夏控制区。

⑧胡虏：对入侵之敌的蔑称，这里指金兵。下文"匈奴"亦同。

⑨天阙：即魏阙，皇宫前的楼观。这里指朝廷。

满 江 红

—— 岳飞

怒发冲冠①，凭栏处，潇潇雨歇。抬望眼，仰天长啸②，壮怀激烈。三十功名尘与土③，八千里路云和月④。莫等闲白了少年头⑤，空悲切！

靖康耻⑥，犹未雪；臣子恨，何时灭？驾长车踏破贺兰山缺⑦。壮志饥餐胡虏肉⑧，笑谈渴饮匈奴血。待从头收拾旧山河，朝天阙⑨。

The Festival of Pure Brightness on the River by Zhang Zeduan, Northern Song, handscroll, color on silk, 24.8 x 528.7 cm, kept in the Palace Museum of Beijing. It's the most renowned piece of genre painting in the history of China's fine arts, delineating the metropolitan life on both sides of the Bianhe River in the Northern Song capital Kaifeng during the Qingming (Pure Brightness) Festival. The artist portrayed a total of about 550 characters, 50 to 60 heads of livestock, some 20 each of carriages, sedan chairs and boats, and about 30 houses, giving a vivid depiction of various aspects of social life. It's of great historical and artistic values.

◎ 清明上河图卷，北宋，张择端，绢本设色，24.8 × 528.7cm，北京故宫博物院藏。这是中国美术史上最为著名的一件风俗画，画的是清明时节北宋都城开封城内外汴河两岸的社会生活图景，总计有人物五百五十余人，牲畜五六十头，车轿船各二十余只，房屋三十余栋，广泛而生动地揭示了当时的工商经济、交通运输的盛况以及民情风俗和各阶层人物的生活状况，具有很高的历史和艺术价值。

TUNE: MORNING HORN AND FROSTY SKY

WRITTEN IN THE PAVILION AT FROWNING CLIFF

— Han Yuanji

A frowning cliff against the sky commands the river from a thousand feet high. On the two far-off browlike peaks with green congealed, how much grief is revealed? Can we express it in excess?

Over angry waves swift blows wind drear; awake from wine, I hear flute songs from the frontier. May I know where is the poet divine? Beyond the green hills in a line, where mist and cloud combine.

shuāng tiān xiǎo jiǎo
霜 天 晓 角

tí cǎi shí é méi tíng ①
题 采 石 蛾 眉 亭

hán yuán jí
——韩 元 吉

yǐ tiān jué bì　　zhí xià jiāng qiān chǐ
倚 天 绝 壁 ， 直 下 江 千 尺 。

tiān jì liǎng é níng dài　　chóu yǔ hèn ， jǐ shí
天 际 两 蛾 凝 黛 ， 愁 与 恨 ， 几 时

jí ②
极 ②？

nù cháo fēng zhèng jí　　jiǔ xǐng wén sài
怒 潮 风 正 急 ， 酒 醒 闻 塞

dí 。　 shì wèn zhé xiān hé chù ③　　qīng shān
笛 。 试 问 谪 仙 何 处 ③？ 青 山

wài ，　 yuǎn yān bì
外 ， 远 烟 碧 。

注 释

①采石矶：故址在安徽马鞍山市长江南岸一带，原名生渚矶。有尖角突入江水，向为兵家必争之地。

②此三句以"天际两蛾凝黛"喻人间离愁别恨之深无穷无尽，没有边际和极限。

③谪仙：李白被贬谪曾称自己为"谪仙人"。相传李白在采石矶捉月后骑鲸仙去。

136

Lotus Flower Emerging from Water, author unknown, Southern Song, round fan, color on silk, 23.8 x 25.1 cm, kept in the Palace Museum of Beijing. Green leaves set off a lotus flower just emerging from water. An overlook view, it shows the graceful flower that emerges unsullied from the filth below. It's an outstanding imperial-court decorative painting.

◎ 出水芙蓉图页，南宋，无款，绢本设色，23.8 × 25.1cm，北京故宫博物院藏。此图绘出水荷花一朵，淡红色晕染，花下衬以绿叶，叶下荷梗三枝。画家用俯视特写的手法，描绘出荷花的雍容外貌和出淤泥而不染的特质。全图笔法精工，设色艳丽，不见墨笔勾痕，是南宋院体画中的精品。

TUNE: PURE SERENE MUSIC
A SUMMER DAY ON THE LAKE

— Zhu Shuzhen

Annoying mist and enticing dew retain me for a while with puzzling view. Hand in hand, we stroll by the Lake of Lotus Flower; a sudden rain drizzles into a shower.

Fond to be silly, I care not for others, never. Undoffed, I lie down with my breast against his chest. What can I do when comes the time to sever? Indolent when back, by my dresser I won't rest.

qīng píng yuè
清 平 乐

xià rì yóu hú
夏 日 游 湖

zhū shū zhēn
—— 朱 淑 真

nǎo yān liāo lù   liú wǒ xū yú
恼 烟 撩 露 ， 留 我 须 臾

zhù   xié shǒu ǒu huā hú shàng lù,   yī
住 。① 携 手 藕 花 湖 上 路 ， 一

shà huāng méi xì yǔ
霎 黄 梅 细 雨 。

jiāo chī bú pà rén cāi   hé yī
娇 痴 不 怕 人 猜 ， 和 衣

shuì dǎo rén huái   zuì shì fēn xié shí hòu,
睡 倒 人 怀 。 最 是 分 携 时 候 ，

guī lái lǎn bàng zhuāng tái
归 来 懒 傍 妆 台 ②。

注 释

① "恼烟"二句：一对初恋的少男少女在西湖谈情说爱，不料恼人的梅雨撩烟拔露，似留人小住。
② "最是"二句：初恋的感觉十分强烈，以致于她与他分手后，还心荡神迷。

Lotus Flower, author unknown, Southern Song, round fan, color on silk, 25.8 x 25 cm, kept in Shanghai Museum. It's a close-up of a lotus flower. The unknown artist abandoned the petals' bounding outlines in favor of sweeping washes of wet ink, and delineated the veins with fine golden lines, adding a peculiar charm to the painting.

◎ 荷花图，佚名，团扇，绢本设色，25.8 × 25cm，上海博物馆藏。此图近写一枝荷花，工细精制。莲瓣以粉罩染，又以桃红由瓣尖晕染。以金丝细线勾勒花瓣的脉络纹路。用笔精细，将风中之荷表现得光华灼灼、流光溢彩，别具风姿。

TUNR: AT THE GOLDEN GATE
MID-SPRING

— Zhu Shuzhen

Half spring has passed, the view awakes a sorrow vague and vast. Unoccupied, I lean on all twelve balustrades, but Heaven cares not if my sorrow fades.

Although the sun is warm and the breeze fair,I envy orioles and swallows in pair. When courtyard flowers fall, I won't uproll the screen; my heart would break when green grass can't be seen.

注 释

①输与：让给。莺莺燕燕：指春天里的黄莺和紫燕。此句是诗人写一佳人毫无心绪欣赏明媚的春光，只好让黄莺紫燕去尽情消受了。

yè jīn mén
谒金门

chūn bàn
春半

zhū shū zhēn
—— 朱淑真

chūn yǐ bàn　　chù mù cǐ qíng wú
春已半，触目此情无

xiàn　　shí èr lán gān xián yǐ biàn　　chóu lái
限。十二阑干闲倚遍，愁来

tiān bù guǎn
天不管。

hǎo shì fēng hé rì nuǎn　　shū yǔ yīng
好是风和日暖，输与莺

yīng yàn yàn ①　　mǎn yuàn luò huā lián bù
莺燕燕①。满院落花帘不

juǎn　　duàn cháng fāng cǎo yuǎn
卷，断肠芳草远。

140

One Hundred Children at Play (partial) by Su Hanchen, Southern Song, handscroll, color on silk, 30.6 x 525.5 cm, kept in the Palace Museum of Taipei. In the painting seven boys view a bamboo picture while two other younger ones are playing nearby. A figure painter. Su was especially good at portraying children's life.

◎ 长春百子（局部），南宋，苏汉臣，绢本设色，30.6 × 525.5cm（卷），台北故宫博物院藏。苏汉臣专长人物画，尤善描写儿童生活。画面描写了稍大的儿童正在欣赏一幅绘画作品，两个稍小的儿童在一旁嬉戏的情景，儿童的表情各异，非常生动，情趣盎然。

141

TUNE: ROUGED LIPS
MEETING WITH AN OLD FRIEND
ON THE WAY

— Zhao Yanduan

Languid at the earth's end, I relive the bygone days when I meet an old friend. So soon I part with you. Can I bear to sing the song of adieu?

A roamer in an alien land, to another roamer I wave my hand. With baseless grief, I turn my head to hear the cicada sings; I see the setting sun red through their dark wings.

diǎn jiàng chún
点 绛 唇

tú zhōng féng guǎn tōng pàn
途 中 逢 管 通 判

zhào yàn duān
—— 赵 彦 端

qiáo cuì tiān yá   gù rén xiāng féng qíng
憔 悴 天 涯 ， 故 人 相 逢 情
rú gù   bié lí hé jù ①   rěn chàng yáng
如 故 。 别 离 何 遽 ① ？ 忍 唱 阳
guān jù ②
关 句 ② ？

wǒ shì xíng rén   gèng sòng xíng rén
我 是 行 人 ， 更 送 行 人
qù   chóu wú jù ③   hán chán míng chù   huí
去 。 愁 无 据 ③ ， 寒 蝉 鸣 处 ， 回
shǒu xié yáng mù
首 斜 阳 暮 。

注 释

①遽：迅速。

②阳关：指古曲"阳关三叠"，此曲曲调哀怨，多在离别时弹奏。

③此三句写作者的无端忧愁无边无际，也许是因为他自己已是旅人，又要送别友人离去的缘故吧！入秋后寒蝉啼叫，回首已夕阳西下。

The Sixth Patriarch Chopping Bamboo by Liang Kai, Southern Song, hanging scroll, ink on paper, 73 x 31.8 cm, kept in the National Museum of Tokyo, Japan. Many of Liang's figure paintings drew materials from Buddhist stories. Hui-neng, the sixth patriarch of the Chan sect of Buddhism in ancient China, is chopping bamboo in the picture. It was drawn in bold lines and a simple, unsophisticated style.

◎ 六祖斫竹图轴，南宋，梁楷，纸本墨笔，73 × 31.8cm，日本东京国立博物馆藏。梁楷的人物画多以佛教禅宗人物或文人雅士为题材，这幅《六祖斫竹图》以顿挫有力富有节奏感的线描表现禅宗六祖慧能砍竹的情态，人物草草数笔而神气迥出，紧张、激昂的情绪从画面中冲泻而出，观者似乎能从那顿挫和跃动的线条中，感受到砍竹发出的声响。

TUNE: RIPPLES SIFTING SAND

AT A FAREWELL BANQUET
IN THE PAVILION OF FLOATING JADE

—Lu You

Green trees darken the Pavilion long; I drink adieu once and again. Often I hate to hear the farewell song, not to say of the autumn day when I'm to go far, far away.

Silk scarfs wet with tears flowing, each of us is broken-hearted. How could a riverful of parting grief be parted? Where could I find the river-barring iron chain to stop the grief from overflowing!

注 释

①尊：同樽。酒杯。

②阳关：指"阳关三叠"。此曲因曲调凄凉使人不忍听。

③"清泪"句：将流出的一行清泪擦拭于罗巾之上。

④"一江"句：离愁别恨充溢于江水，两位离人恰可平分此间愁情。

⑤"安得"二句：怎么才能得到横截于江面的巨大铁锁来锁住穷愁迷雾的渡口，使人不再忧愁？津：渡口。

làng táo shā
浪 淘 沙

dān yáng fú yù tíng xí shàng zuò
丹 阳 浮 玉 亭 席 上 作

lù yóu
——陆 游

lù shù àn cháng tíng　　jǐ bǎ lí zūn
绿 树 暗 长 亭 ， 几 把 离 尊 ①。

yáng guān cháng hèn bù kān wén　　hé kuàng jīn zhāo
阳 关 常 恨 不 堪 闻 ②， 何 况 今 朝

qiū sè lǐ　　shēn shì xíng rén
秋 色 里 ， 身 是 行 人 。

qíng lèi yì luó jīn　　gē zì xiāo hún
清 泪 挹 罗 巾 ③， 各 自 销 魂 。

yì jiāng lí hèn qià píng fēn　　ān dé qiān xún
一 江 离 恨 恰 平 分 ④。 安 得 千 寻

héng tiě suǒ　　jié duàn yān jīn
横 铁 锁 ， 截 断 烟 津 ⑤？

144

Bamboo and Sparrow by Wu Bing, Southern Song, album leaf, color on silk, 25 x 25 cm, kept in Shanghai Museum. It's a representative work of the painter. A sparrow on a bamboo twig is grooming its feathers. The bird was drawn in colors directly without first making sketches.

◎ 竹雀图页，南宋，吴炳，绢本设色，25 × 25cm，上海博物馆藏。此图写棘竹丛生，枝桠横出，枝头有一只麻雀正悠闲地啄理羽毛。整幅画景物居于下侧，可见南宋构图新风的影响。图中主枝用双钩技法，雀鸟用色彩没骨画出后，重点部位再用墨线描出。这是吴炳传世作品中的代表作。

TUNE: PHOENIX HAIRPIN

—Lu You

Pink hands so fine, gold-branded wine, spring paints the willows green palace walls can't confine. East wind unfair, happy times rare. In my heart sad thoughts throng; we've severed for years long. Wrong, wrong, wrong!

Spring is as green, in vain she's lean. Her kerchief soaked with tears and red with stains unclean. Peach blossoms fall near deserted hall. Our oath is still there. Lo! No words to her can go. No, no, no!

注 释

①红酥手：形容手的肤色如酥油一样红润细嫩。

②黄藤酒：即黄封酒。宋法，京师官酒，以黄罗绢封缠瓶口，名黄封酒。

③离索：离散。索：散。

④红：指泪水浸胭脂而染红。浥：沾湿。鲛绡：神话中人鱼（鲛人）所织的纱绢，这里指手帕。

⑤莫，莫，莫：罢，罢，罢。一说"错莫"为互文，落寞之意。李白《赠别从甥高五》："三朝空错莫，对饮却惭冤。"

chāi tóu fēng
钗头凤

—— lù yóu
陆游

hóng sū shǒu ①，huáng téng jiǔ ②，mǎn chéng chūn
红 酥 手 ，黄 藤 酒 ，满 城 春
sè gōng qiáng liǔ。dōng fēng è，huān qíng bó。yī
色 宫 墙 柳 。东 风 恶 ，欢 情 薄 。一
huái chóu xù，jǐ nián lí suǒ ③。cuò，cuò，
怀 愁 绪 ，几 年 离 索 。错 ，错 ，
cuò
错 ！

chūn rú jiù，rén kōng shòu，lèi hén hóng yì
春 如 旧 ，人 空 瘦 ，泪 痕 红 浥
jiāo xiāo tòu ④。táo huā luò，xián chí gé。shān méng
鲛 绡 透 。桃 花 落 ，闲 池 阁 。山 盟
suī zài，jǐn shū nán tuō。mò，mò，mò ⑤！
虽 在 ，锦 书 难 托 。莫 ，莫 ，莫 ！

146

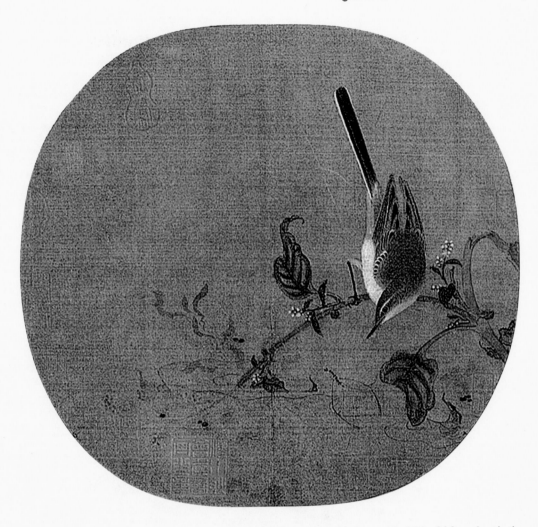

Water Bird on Knotweed, author unknown, Southern Song, round fan, color on silk, 25.2 x 26.8 cm, kept in the Palace Museum of Beijing. A water bird standing on knotweed looks down at swimming shrimps. The bird's feathers were delineated with fine, delicate touches.

◎ 红蓼水禽图页，南宋，无款，绢本设色，25.2 × 26.8cm，北京故宫博物院藏。此图画红蓼一枝，枝头向左浸入水中，枝上蓼花朵朵，蓼叶扶持。一禽栖于蓼枝间，双眼下窥水中游虾。鸟的羽毛用细笔勾描，形象生动活泼。全图笔法精秀，设色妍美，构图别致，写实水平极高。

TUNE: PHOENIX HAIRPIN

— Tang Wan

The world unfair, true manhood rare. Dusk melts away in rain and blooming trees turn bare. Morning wind high, tear traces dry. I'd write to him what's in my heart; leaning on rails, I speak apart. Hard, hard, hard!

Go each our ways! Gone are our days. My sick soul groans like ropes of swing which sways. The horn blows cold; night has grown old. Afraid my grief may be descried, I try to hide my tears undried. Hide, hide, hide!

chāi tóu fèng
钗头凤

tāng wǎn
—— 唐婉

shì qíng bó　　rén qíng è　　　yǔ sòng huáng
世 情 薄 ， 人 情 恶 ， 雨 送 黄
hūn huā yì luò　　wǎn fēng gān　　lèi hén cán
昏 花 易 落 。 晚 风 干 ， 泪 痕 残 。
yù jiān xīn shì ①　　dú yǔ xié lán　　nán
欲 笺 心 事 ① ， 独 语 斜 阑 。 难 ，
nán　　nán
难 ， 难 ！

rén chéng gè ②　　jīn fēi zuó　　bìng hún
人 成 各 ② ， 今 非 昨 ， 病 魂
cháng sì qiū qiān suǒ ③　　jiǎo shēng hán　　yè lán
常 似 秋 千 索 ③ 。 角 声 寒 ， 夜 阑
shān ④　　pà rén xún wèn　　yàn lèi zhuāng huān
珊 ④ 。 怕 人 寻 问 ， 咽 泪 装 欢 。
mán　　mán　　mán
瞒 ， 瞒 ， 瞒 ！

注 释

① 欲笺心事：想要将心里的感触写于彩笺寄给爱人。

② 人成各：即人落单，各自分飞。

③ 病魂：痛苦的心灵。此句形容自己心神恍惚，动荡不安。

④ 阑珊：将尽。

Withered Tree and a Mynah, author unknown, Song Dynasty, round fan, color on silk, 25 x 26.5 cm, kept in the Palace Museum of Beijing. A mynah is resting in an autumn tree with dead twigs and withered leaves. It's an outstanding flower-and-bird painting.

◎ 枯树鸲鹆图，佚名，团扇，绢本设色，25 × 26.5cm，北京故宫博物院藏。鸲鹆，即八哥，是富贵之家笼养的一种能学人言的鸟儿。此图作秋树残叶，枯枝上栖息着一只八哥。整幅构图疏密得体，用笔工整，形神兼备，不失为宋代写生花鸟画的杰作。然而残叶枯枝，纵有可人的鸟儿立于其间，又岂能不使人产生伤时感世之情呢。

精选

宋词与宋画

TUNE: DREAMLIKE SONG

— Yan Rui

What's wrong with flowers of the pear? What's wrong with the apricot fair? They are so red and white, so red and white that the east wind is drunk with delight. Do not forget, do not forget, tipsy on Peach Blossom Land, my sleeves were wet!

如梦令
rú mèng lìng

—— 严蕊
yān ruǐ

道是梨花不是，道是
dào shì lí huā bú shì dào shì

杏花不是。白白与红红，别
xìng huā bú shì bái bái yǔ hóng hóng bié

是东风情味。曾记，曾记人
shì dōng fēng qíng wèi céng jì céng jì rén

在武陵微醉①。
zài wǔ líng wēi zuì

150

Winter Play (partial) by Su Hanchen, Southern Song, hanging scroll, color on silk, 196.2 x 107.1 cm, kept in the Palace Museum of Taipei. In the painting, elder sister and younger brother, with a small flag and a peacock feather in their hands, are playing with a cat in their courtyard.

◎ 冬日婴戏（局部），南宋，苏汉臣，绢本设色，196.2 × 107.1cm(轴)，台北故宫博物院藏。苏汉臣专长人物画，尤善描写儿童生活。这幅画描绘了姐弟二人在庭院里玩耍的情景，姐姐手执一根色彩斑斓的旗子，弟弟则用一根红绳牵着一根孔雀翎。两人都看着左下角的一只小猫，小猫毛色亮丽，动作活泼可爱。

TUNE: GROPING FOR FISH

— Xin Qiji

How much more can spring bear of wind and rain? Too hastily it will leave again. Lovers of spring would fear to see the flowers red budding too soon and fallen petals too widespread. O spring, please stay! I've heard it said that sweet grass far away would stop you from seeing your returning way. But I've not heard spring say a word. Only the busy spider weaves webs all day long by painted eaves to keep the willow down from taking leave.

Could a disfavored consort again to favor rise? Could beauty not be envied by green eyes? Even if favor could be bought back again, to whom of this unanswered love can she complain? Do not dance then! Have you not seen both plump and slender beauties turn to dust? Bitter grief is just that you can't do what you want to. Oh, do not lean on overhanging rails where the setting sun sees heartbroken willow trees!

宿雨清畿旬
朝陽麗帝城
豐年人樂業
隴上踏歌行

Tage (*Walking While Singing*) by Ma Yuan, Southern Song, hanging scroll, color on silk, 192.5 x 111 cm, kept in the Palace Museum of Beijing. Ma tended to draw landscape in a simple way. In this scroll, the distant view shows several mountain peaks soaring into the sky; in the foreground, on a mountain path walk some drunken farmers. Swaying slender bamboos and willow twigs on the roadside indicate that spring is very much in the air.

◎ 踏歌图轴，南宋，马远，绢本设色，192.5×111cm，北京故宫博物院藏。马远作画喜欢表现山水之一角，画面景物通常是简到不能再简，故在画史上有"马一角"之称。这幅《踏歌图》中，远处为几座危耸的山峰，清瘦坚硬，直插云霄。石峰上又有松杉挺立，更显秀美。山下衬以蓊郁的松杉，云雾缭绕中有楼阁隐现。下半部近景是一条穿插在山石间的小路，迎风摇曳的修竹和柳丝，带给人一屡春意，而路上老农的醉态和童心表现得也都非常生动，正是一年初春踏歌时节的好闲暇。

摸鱼儿

—— 辛弃疾

更能消几番风雨？匆匆春又归去①。惜春长怕花开早，何况落红无数②！春且住！见说道，天涯芳草无归路。怨春不语③。算只有殷勤，画檐蛛网，尽日惹飞絮④。

长门事，准拟佳期又误。娥眉曾有人妒。千金纵买相如赋，默默此情谁诉⑤？君莫舞！君不见，玉环飞燕皆尘土⑥？闲愁最苦。休去倚危栏！斜阳正在烟柳断肠处。

注 释

①"更能"二句：春天还能消受几番风雨的袭击，便要真的归去了。

②"惜春"二句：写作者惜春的心情。"落红无数"又引出了他的伤春情绪。

③"春且住"四句：春天，你且留住吧，听说，天边长满了芳草，春天的去路已被堵塞。人怨恨春之无情，春却不语。

④"算只有"三句：想想人无计留春，还不如画檐下的蜘蛛，殷勤织网，却还能粘住扬花无数。

⑤"长门事"五句：用汉武帝陈皇后失宠的典故，来比拟自己政途的失意。陈皇后被打入冷宫，是因遭人嫉妒。她后来用黄金买得司马相如的《长安赋》，希望它能打动汉武帝的心，但她的期望终归落空，"佳期"难再。这种痛苦，自己能向谁倾诉呢。

⑥"君莫舞"三句：那时妒忌别人向君王邀宠的人，也不要再玩弄你们的伎俩暗自高兴了。你们没有见到杨玉环和赵飞燕后来不是都死于非命，灰飞烟灭了吗？

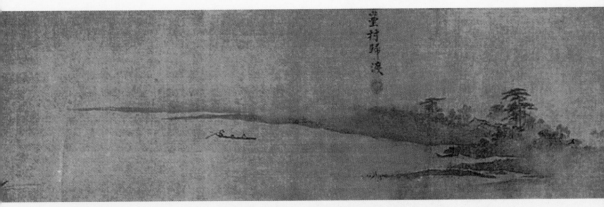

Twelve Views from a Thatched Hut, ascribed to Xia Gui, Southern Song, color on silk, kept in the Nelson-Atkins Museum of Art, U.S.A. Legend goes that Xia drew 12 landscape pictures, but only four of them are extant. The artist used well-arranged composition and succinct style to create a lofty artistic ambience.

◎ 山水十二图卷（四景），南宋，夏圭（传），绢本设色，美国纳尔逊－艾金斯美术馆藏。相传为夏圭所作的《山水十二段》，表现了不同景色的山水十二种风景，现仅存其四：遥天书雁、烟村归渡、渔笛清幽、烟堤晚泊。画家通过对雁阵飞向辽远天际的描绘，将各段间自然联为一体，以其精炼的画面和巧妙的构图，表现出渔笛悠扬、如诗如幻的审美境界。

TUNE: PURE SERENE MUSIC

— Xin Qiji

The thatched roof slants low, beside the brook green grasses grow. Who talks with drunken Southern voice to please? White-haired man and wife at their ease.

East of the brook their eldest son is hoeing weeds; their second son now makes a cage for hens he feeds. How pleasant to see their spoiled youngest son who heeds nothing but lies by brookside and pods lotus seeds!

注 释

①茅檐低小：茅草盖的房檐又底又矮，首句点明这里是一处农家。
②吴音：吴地方音，指江苏苏州一带的口音。相媚好，指言语亲切婉转。
③翁媪：年老的男人和女人。
④无赖：淘气的情态。
⑤卧剥莲蓬：卧伏在那里剥弃莲蓬。

清平乐 (qīng píng yuè)

—— 辛弃疾 (xīn qì jí)

茅檐低小①，溪上青青草。醉里吴音相媚好②，白发谁家翁媪③？

大儿锄豆溪东，中儿正织鸡笼。最喜小儿无赖④，溪头卧剥莲蓬⑤。

One Hundred Children at Play (partial) by Su Hanchen, Southern Song, handscroll, color on silk, 30.6 x 525.5 cm, kept in the Palace Museum of Taipei. In the painting a kid stands on the bank of a pond, while his pal, naked, is plucking a lotus flower in it.

◎ 长春百子（局部），南宋，苏汉臣，绢本设色，30.6 × 525.5cm（卷），台北故宫博物院藏。此图描绘两个儿童一个站在水塘边上，一个光着身子正在池塘里采荷花。画面柔和，用笔清丽，表现了画家细致的观察能力、高度的概括能力以及精深的笔墨表现能力。

TUNE: THE MOON OVER THE WEST RIVER

HOME-GOING AT NIGHT FROM THE YELLOW SAND BRIDGE

— Xin Qiji

Startled by magpies leaving the branch in moonlight, I hear cicadas shrill in the breeze at midnight. The ricefields' sweet smell promises a bumper year. Listen, how frogs' croaks please the ear!

Beyond the clouds seven or eight stars twinkle; before the hills two or three raindrops sprinkle. There is an inn beside the village temple. Look! The winding path leads to the hut beside the brook.

xī jiāng yuè
西 江 月

yè xíng huáng shā dào zhōng
夜 行 黄 沙 道 中

xīn qì jí
—— 辛 弃 疾

míng yuè bié zhī jīng què   qīng fēng bàn
明 月 别 枝 惊 鹊 ， 清 风 半

yè míng chán ①   dào huā xiāng lǐ shuō fēng nián
夜 鸣 蝉 。 稻 花 香 里 说 丰 年 ，

tīng qǔ wā shēng yí piàn
听 取 蛙 声 一 片 。

qī bā gè xīng tiān wài   liǎng sān diǎn
七 八 个 星 天 外 ， 两 三 点

yǔ shān qián   jiù shí máo diàn shè lín biān
雨 山 前 。 旧 时 茅 店 社 林 边 ，

lù zhuǎn xī qiáo hū xiàn ②
路 转 溪 桥 忽 现 。

注 释

① "明月" 二句：清风、明月之夜清幽舒爽。鸟鹊择枝惊飞，加上夜半蝉鸣，使这个静谧的夏夜多了一些生机。

② "旧时" 二句：作者在转过溪上小桥时，惊喜地发现了一家过去熟识的茅屋小店在社庙旁的树林间。社林，土地庙旁边的树林。

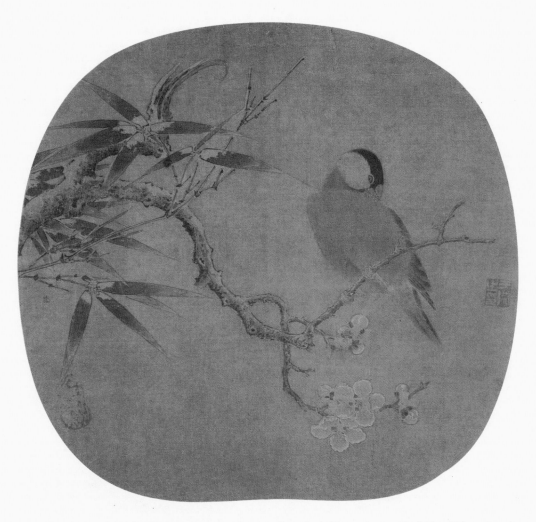

Plum, Bamboo and Winter Bird by Lin Chun, Southern Song, round fan, color on silk, 24.8 x 26.9 cm, kept in Shanghai Museum. In the thawing snow, a bird is grooming its feathers on a plum branch. The fresh artistic conception produced in this picture can also be found in the literary works of Jiang Kui, a Southern Song *ci* poet.

◎ 梅竹寒禽图，林椿，团扇，绢本设色，24.8 × 26.9cm，上海博物馆藏。此图写残雪未消之际，寒雀刷羽梅花枝头，竹梅为双钩填彩，而雀则用细毫写羽毛，写实逼真。雪梅疏竹，天地寂寂，莫不是江国月色，夜雪初积之时，这鸟儿正陶醉在梅边笛声里么？词人姜夔有 "但怪得、竹外疏花，香冷入瑶席" 之佳句，岂不正是这等意境的写照吗？

TUNE: SONG OF UGLY SLAVE

WRITTEN ON THE WALL ON
MY WAY TO BOSHAN

— Xin Qiji

While young, I knew no grief I could not bear;

I'd like to go upstair. I'd like to go upstair to write

new verses with a false despair.

I know what grief is now that I am old; I would

not have it told. I would not have it told, but only say

I'm glad that autumn's cold.

注　释

①"为赋"句：为了赋出新词硬说自己忧愁。这是少年人无病呻吟的一种姿态，很符合少年时的境况。

②"却道"句：与前对比，作者历尽人生的沧桑后，特别是心怀报国无门的悲愤之后，再也不想对人诉说心中的愁苦，郁闷无处发泄，只有自我消解。登上层楼后，只说天气凉了，好一个秋天啊！

chǒu nú ér
丑 奴 儿

shū bó shān dào zhōng bì
书 博 山 道 中 壁

xīn qì jí
——辛弃疾

shào nián bù shí chóu zī wèi　　　　ài shàng
少 年 不 识 愁 滋 味 ，　爱 上

céng lóu　　　ài shàng céng lóu　　wèi fù xīn cí
层 楼 。 爱 上 层 楼 ， 为 赋 新 词

qiǎng shuō chóu
强 说 愁 ①。

ér jīn shí jìn chóu zī wèi　　　　yù shuō
而 今 识 尽 愁 滋 味 ，　欲 说

huán xiū　　　yù shuō huán xiū　　què dào tiān liáng
还 休 。 欲 说 还 休 ， 却 道 天 凉

hǎo gè qiū
好 个 秋 ②。

Plums, Rocks, Stream and Wild Ducks by Ma Yuan, Southern Song, album leaf, color on silk, 26.7 x 28.6 cm, kept in the Palace Museum of Beijing. Ma inherited and further developed Li Tang's drawing technique. He's expert in showing the shades and texture of rocks and mountains by light ink strokes. In this picture a large blank space was left to set off the landscape, reflecting Ma's typical style.

◎ 梅石溪凫图页，南宋，马远，绢本设色，26.7 × 28.6cm，北京故宫博物院藏。马远继承并发展了李唐的画风，擅长以雄健的大斧劈皴画奇峭坚实的山石峰峦，以托枝的多姿形态画梅树，尤善于在章法上大胆取舍剪裁，在画面上留出大面积空白以突出景观，表现空濛的空间及浓郁的诗意。这幅《梅石溪凫图页》，反映了马远的典型画风。

TUNE: WATER DRAGON CHANT

ON RIVERSIDE TOWER AT JIANKANG

— Xin Qiji

The southern sky for miles and miles in autumn dye and boundless autumn water spread to meet the sky. I gaze on far-off northern hills like spiral shells or hair decor of jade, which grief or hatred overfills. Leaning at sunset on balustrade and hearing a lonely swan's song, a wanderer on southern land, I look at my precious sword long, and pound all the railings with my hand, but nobody knows why I climb the tower high.

Don't say for food the perch is good! When west winds blow, why don't I homeward go? I'd be ashamed to see the patriot, should I retire to seek for land and cot. I sigh for passing years I can't retain; in driving wind and blinding rain even an old tree grieves. To whom then may I say to wipe my tears away with her pink handkerchief or her green sleeves?

Chicks to Be Fed by Li Di, Southern Song, album leaf, color on silk, 23.7 x 24.6 cm, kept in the Palace Museum of Beijing. In the picture two chickens are crying for food. The painter didn't set any background image. Two chickens drawn with fine touches in three colors look lovely.

◎ 鸡雏待饲图页，南宋，李迪，绢本设色，23.7 × 24.6cm，北京故宫博物院藏。此图设色画鸡雏两只，一只站立昂首，一只半卧状，均张口嘶叫，等待喂食。画面不作背景，以黑、白、黄三色细笔勾描鸡雏细润丰满的羽毛，神情十分生动，逗人喜爱。

水龙吟

登建康赏心亭①

——辛弃疾

楚天千里清秋，水随天去秋无际。遥岑远目②，献愁供恨③，玉簪螺髻④。落日楼头，断鸿声里，江南游子，把吴钩看了⑤，栏杆拍遍，无人会登临意。

休说鲈鱼堪脍⑥，尽西风，季鹰归未⑦？求田问舍⑧，怕应羞见刘郎才气。可惜流年，忧愁风雨，树犹如此⑨。倩何人唤取红巾翠袖，揾英雄泪⑩？

注 释

①建康：南京的旧称。赏心亭：北宋时建，下临秦淮河，可以观览周边景致。

②遥岑远目：远望群山。岑，山。远目，远远地看去。

③献愁供恨：指这里的山水让人一见便心有所恨。

④玉簪螺髻：形容远山如美人的玉簪与螺旋形发髻般秀丽。

⑤吴钩：宝刀。

⑥脍：将鱼肉切成细片。

⑦季鹰：西晋张翰字。其为官在洛阳时，见秋风起，便想到家乡吴中的莼菜羹、鲈鱼脍，便以此为借口弃官而去。

⑧求田问舍：喻胸无大志。求田，买田。问舍，盖房。

⑨树犹如此：东晋桓温北伐，见昔年种柳，柳粗十围。曾叹曰："木犹如此，人何以堪"。

⑩红巾翠袖：指歌妓。揾：擦。

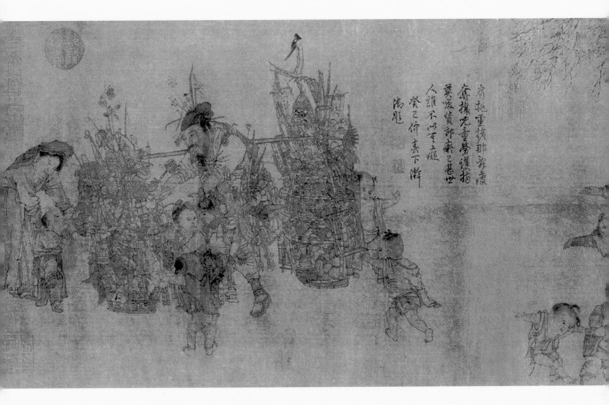

An Itinerant Pedlar (partial) by Li Song, Southern Song, handscroll, light color on silk, 25.5 x 70.4 cm, kept in the Palace Museum of Beijing. The Song Dynasty genre painting vividly depicts the life of people living at the bottom of society. Though being held in contempt by the later literati artists, it indeed holds an important position in the history of China's fine arts. This scroll is a representative work of the Song Dynasty genre painting, permeated with a strong flavor of rural life.

◎ 货郎图（局部），南宋，李嵩，绢本淡设色，25.5 × 70.4cm，北京故宫博物院藏。宋代的风俗画在中国美术史上独具特色，往往以生动的形象来描绘社会底层的生活，虽然因反映了市民的欣赏趣味而为后世文人不屑，但就其对人物个性描绘所达到的艺术高度来看，又在中国绘画中占有重要地位。李嵩的这件《货郎图》，就是传世的宋代风俗画中的代表作，图中对货郎担上各种货物刻画之精巧，生活气息之浓郁，历来为人们惊叹。

TUNE: SONG OF IMMORTALS

FAREWELL TO MY LOVE

— Liu Guo

It's easy to get drunk with wine of adieu. Turning my head, I find thirty miles out of view. My steed won't stop but fly from mile to mile; I hold its halter for a while, and sit down for a while. What can I do when severed by hills and rills from you!

Though glorious task should be undertaken, how can love be forsaken? The streamer of mist-veiled wineshop slants away. I may forward go, or I may stay. To go or stay is for you as for me the same woe.

tiān xiān zǐ
天 仙 子

chū fù shěng bié qiè yú sān shí lǐ tóu
初 赴 省 别 妾 于 三 十 里 头

liú guò
—— 刘过

bié jiǔ xūn xūn hún yì zuì ① huí guò
别 酒 醺 醺 浑 易 醉 ①， 回 过
tóu lái sān shí lǐ mǎ ér bù zhù qù rú
头 来 三 十 里 。 马 儿 不 住 去 如
fēi qiān yì qì ② zuò yì qì duàn sòng shà
飞 ， 牵 一 憩 ②， 坐 一 憩 ， 断 送 煞
rén shān yǔ shuǐ ③
人 山 与 水 。
shì zé shì gōng míng zhōng kě xǐ bú dào
是 则 是 功 名 终 可 喜 ， 不 道
ēn qíng pàn dé wèi ④ yún mí cūn diàn jiǔ qí
恩 情 拚 得 未 ④！ 云 迷 村 店 酒 旗
xié qù yě shì zhù yě shì fán nǎo zì
斜 。 去 也 是 ， 住 也 是 ， 烦 恼 自
jiā fán nǎo nǐ
家 烦 恼 你 。

注 释

① 醺醺：形容酒醉的样子。

② 憩：休息。

③ 煞：用在动词后，表示极度。

④ 拚：舍弃。此指恩爱能够舍弃得了吗？

166

Hawk and Pheasant by Li Di, Southern Song, hanging scroll, color on silk, 189.4 x 210 cm, kept in the Palace Museum of Beijing. A ferocious hawk on a maple branch stares at a fleeing pheasant, preparing to dash at it at any moment. The painter drew the old tree and rocks with heavy strokes. It's a very dynamic painting.

◎ 枫鹰雉鸡图轴，南宋，李迪，绢本设色，189.4 × 210cm，北京故宫博物院藏。此图以巨幅绘坡石竹丛中，一棵古枫拔地而起，枯枝上一只凶猛的苍鹰正怒视着一只慌忙逃窜的雉鸡。画面上的山石树干用笔粗重，辅以水墨皴染，其阴阳向背，都交待得十分清楚。树上的枝叶疏密有致，层次鲜明。鹰之蓄势待发与雉之仓皇胆寒，都刻画得十分准确生动。

TUNE: ROUGED LIPS

PASSING BY WUSONG
IN THE WINTER OF 1187

— Jiang Kui

The heartless swallows and wild geese fly away west of the lake with the cloud and breeze. Peak on peak grizzles in dread of evening drizzles.

Beside the Fourth Bridge, I would follow poets of days gone by. How are they today? Leaning on rails, I sigh, high and low withered willows swing and sway.

diǎn jiāng chún
点 绛 唇

dīng wèi dōng guò wú sōng zuò
丁 未 冬 过 吴 松 作

— Jiang kui
—— 姜 夔

yān yàn wú xīn ①   tài hú xī pàn
燕 雁 无 心 ,   太 湖 西 畔
suí yún qù   shù fēng qīng kǔ   shāng lüè huáng
随 云 去 。   数 峰 清 苦 ,   商 略 黄
hūn yǔ ②
昏 雨 。

dì sì qiáo biān ③   nǐ gòng tiān suí
第 四 桥 边 ,   拟 共 天 随
zhù ④   jīn hé xǔ   píng lán huái gǔ
住 。   今 何 许 ?   凭 阑 怀 古 ,
cán liǔ cēn cī wǔ ⑤
残 柳 参 差 舞 。

精选
宋词
与
宋画

注 释

①燕雁：北方的大雁。
②商略：商量，酝酿。
③第四桥：据载为吴江城外的甘泉桥。因泉水品质而位居第四。陆龟蒙曾主在此地。
④天随：唐朝诗人陆龟蒙自号天随子。姜白石心仪于陆龟蒙，借此表达自己飘泊的人生毫无心机，纯任天然。
⑤参差：柳质纤弱，何况又残，因此舞起来会参差不齐。

168

Grazing and the Landscape by Qi Xu, Northern Song, handscroll, color on silk, 47.3 x 115.6 cm, kept in the Palace Museum of Beijing. Qi was Emperor Zhenzong's court painter, and this is his only work left behind. In the early years of the Northern Song, a majority of the paintings covered political or religious subjects, while landscape paintings were relatively seldom seen. This scroll depicts the grazing scene in south China, revealing a peaceful and auspicious atmosphere.

◎ 江山放牧图卷，北宋，祁序，绢本设色，47.3 × 115.6cm，北京故宫博物院藏。祁序为宋真宗时的画院待诏，生平经历已不可考，仅有这一幅作品传世。由于绘画"宣教"的功能，北宋早期的宫廷绘画，以政治、宗教为内容的作品仍占主流，单纯用作欣赏的花鸟、山水等自然景物为题材的作品，虽有而不多见。祁序的这件作品，描绘了江南放牧的自然景色，应当是为了歌颂天下升平而作，但其中所流露的恬淡祥和的气象，却深得文人之旨趣。

TUNE: PARTRIDGE IN THE SKY

A DREAM ON THE NIGHT OF LANTERN FESTIVAL

—Jiang Kui

The endless River Fei to the east keeps on flowing; the love seed we once sowed forever keeps on growing. Your face I saw in dream was not clear to my eyes as in your portrait, soon I am wakened by birds' cries.

Spring not yet green, my grey hair seen, our separation's been too long to grieve the heart. Why make the past reappear before us from year to year on Lantern Festival when we are far apart!

zhè gū tiān

鹧鸪天

yuán yè yǒu suǒ mèng

元夜有所梦①

jiāng kuí

——姜夔

fěi shuǐ dōng liú wú jìn qī dāng chū bù
肥水东流无尽期②，当初不
hé zhǒng xiāng sī mèng zhōng wèi bǐ dān qīng jiàn
合种相思。梦中未比丹青见③，
àn lǐ hū jīng shān niǎo tí
暗里忽惊山鸟啼④。

chūn wèi lǜ bìn xiān sī rén jiān bié jiǔ
春未绿，鬓先丝，人间别久
bù chéng bēi shuí jiāo suì suì hóng lián yè liǎng
不成悲。谁教岁岁红莲夜⑤，两
chù chén yín gè zì zhī
处沉吟各自知。

注 释

①元夜有所梦：有的版本为"元夕有所梦"。这是一首怀念旧日恋人的情词。

②"肥水"句：肥水，即淝水。分东西二支，东流指向东流经合肥入巢湖的一支。此句的无尽期，象征着岁月悠悠中无尽的相思与别恨。

③"梦中"句：梦中所见伊人仿佛没有丹青图画中所见真切。

④"暗里"句：山鸟的啼鸣又使作者幻梦初醒，颇为惆怅。

⑤"谁教"二句：红莲夜，指元宵灯节。元宵佳节应是团圆之节，而作者却与心爱的人天各一方，沉思默想，两地相思。

Bamboos, Rocks and Colorful Birds by Huang Jucai, Northern Song, handscroll, color on silk, 23.6 x 45.7 cm, kept in the Palace Museum of Taipei. A curly oak tree stands by a stream. Some dozen of birds either rest on the tree branches or hunt for food on the waterside. The artist showed the shades and texture of mountain rocks by light ink strokes, and drew the outlines of the bamboos and oak leaves with fine lines and then filled them with color.

◎ 竹石锦鸡图，黄居寀，绢本设色，23.6 × 45.7cm，中国台北故宫博物院藏。秋天栎树凋零，几只鸠雀或停栖在枝头，或在山石、或在水旁觅食啄饮。画面淡雅空濛。山石略加勾点，以皴笔擦出。竹丛栎叶皆以勾填法绘出。几只鸠鸟姿态各异，刻画细致，质感丰厚，显示了黄氏风格。

171

TUNE: SLOW SONG OF YANGZHOU

— Jiang Kui

In the famous town east of River Huai and scenic spot of Bamboo West, breaking my journey, I alight for a short rest. The three-mile splendid road in breeze have I passed by; it's now overgrown with wild green wheat and weeds. Since Northern shore was overrun by Jurchen steeds, even the tall trees beside the pond have been war-torn. As dusk is drawing near, cold blows the born; the empty town looks drear.

The place Du Mu the poet prized, if he should come again today, would render him surprised. His verse on the cardamon spray and on sweet dreams in mansions green could not express my deep distress. The Twenty-four Bridges can still be seen, but the cold moon floating among the waves would no more sing a song. For whom should the peonies near the bridge grow red from year to year?

迎風呈巧媚
浥露逞紅妍

Almond Blossoms by Ma Yuan, Southern Song, album leaf, color on silk, 25.8 x 27.3 cm, kept in the Palace Museum of Taipei. Ma was expert in drawing landscape, figures, flowers and birds. He was ranked along with Xia Gui, Li Tang and Liu Songnian as one of the Four Great Masters of the Southern Song Dynasty. This picture, portraying a spray of almond blossoms, is reminiscent of the painter's skill to leave a stretch of blank space to set off objects from the background, which he adopted often in his well-known landscape paintings.

◎ 倚云仙杏图，马远，册页，绢本设色，25.8 × 27.3cm，中国台北故宫博物院藏。马远擅画山水，兼精人物花鸟，尤工画水，与夏圭、李唐、刘松年并称"南宋四家"。马远擅在章法上取舍裁减，多描绘山之一角水之一涯的局部，常在画面留下大量空白以突出景观，并因此而有浓郁的诗意。此图绘一枝杏花斜伸，独占一角，与他的山水画章法有异曲同工之妙。所不同的是，在本幅作品中，画家以精细工整的笔法，将绽放的杏花表现得有堆粉砌霜之姿、轻灵润秀之趣，堪为花鸟妙品。

扬州慢

yáng zhōu màn

——姜夔

淮左名都①，竹西佳处②，解鞍少驻初程。过春风十里③，尽荠麦青青④。自胡马窥江去后，废池乔木，犹厌言兵。渐黄昏，清角吹寒，都在空城。

杜郎俊赏⑤，算而今重到须惊。纵豆蔻词工⑥，青楼梦好⑦，难赋深情。二十四桥仍在⑧，波心荡，冷月无声。念桥边红药⑨，年年知为谁生！

注 释

①淮左：扬州在淮水东，淮左即淮东。

②竹西：亭名，在扬州蜀冈之西。"谁知竹西路，歌吹是扬州。"见杜牧《题扬州禅智寺》诗。

③春风十里："春风十里扬州路，卷上珠帘总不如"，出杜牧《赠别》诗。此指昔日的繁华。

④尽荠麦青青：到处都长满了野生的麦子，一片荒芜景象。

⑤杜郎：指唐代诗人杜牧。

⑥豆蔻词工："豆蔻梢头二月初"，出杜牧《赠别》诗，用以形容美人的年少。

⑦青楼梦好：杜牧《遣怀》诗："十年一觉扬州梦，赢得青楼薄倖名。"青楼：妓女所居。

⑧二十四桥：唐代扬州有二十四桥。北宋时尚余七座，见沈括《补笔谈》。此处泛用，并非实指。

⑨红药：芍药。

Bony Horse by Gong Kai, Southern Song, handscroll, ink and wash on paper, 29.9 x 56.9 cm, kept in Osaka Municipal Art Museum, Japan. The painter drew a thin and bony but untamed horse to stress the "backbone," or moral courage thought highly of by intellectuals living in the last years of the Southern Song and the early phase of the Yuan Dynasty.

◎ 骏骨图，龚开，纸本水墨，29.9 × 56.9cm，日本大阪市立美术馆藏。龚开绘马，瘦骨嶙峋，意在强调"骨气"，这也是宋末元初文人自诩的一种气节。此马伸颈低首，似伏枥之状；鬃毛飘动，有秋风萧瑟、不胜寒冷之感，而其眼神凛烈，仍寓不屈之态。用笔精到，勾线写骨，鬃毛更是根根写出迎风飘摆之态，造型生动准确。

TUNE: DOFFING THE PENDANTS

— Shi Dazu

Strolling by flower-bed fine, my robe fragrant with dew, I'd confide to spring my verse new. Often would I send my love, but swallows won't carry it above for him to read by pearl screen my clever line.

Deep, deep am I lovesick; my sorrow is thick, thick. How could I forget his whisper by lamplight? Pear blossoms steeped in pale moonlight, I'd come in borrowed dream to gallery by flowers to show him my sleeves wet with tears fallen in showers.

解佩令 (jiě pèi lìng)

—— 史达祖 (shǐ dá zǔ)

人行花坞①，衣沾香雾，有新词逢春分付。屡欲传情，奈燕子不曾飞去，传珠帘咏郎秀句。

相思一度，浓愁一度，最难忘遮灯私语，淡月梨花，借梦来花边廊庑②，指春衫泪曾溅处。

注释

①花坞：四面如屏的百花深处。
②廊庑：堂前的廊屋。

176

Orchids by Zhao Mengjian, Southern Song, handscroll, ink on paper, 34.5 x 90.2 cm, kept in the Palace Museum of Beijing. Most court painters in the Song Dynasty sketched the outlines of bamboos and orchids and then filled them with color. However, Zhao blazed a new path for himself. In this scroll he drew two orchids with freehand brushwork to seek similarity in spirit rather than formal resemblance, which set a new model for later painters to draw orchids.

◎ 墨兰图卷，南宋，赵孟坚，纸本墨笔，34.5 × 90.2cm，北京故宫博物院藏。我们现在能见到两宋时期皇家画院中人画的兰竹，大都用勾线填色之法，但赵孟坚笔下的墨兰，受文人画风的影响，创造了一笔写出的写意之法，也强调了绘画的"意似"，重情态而不重形质，信笔挥洒而就，突出了审美情绪的自然表露，为后世的墨兰画树立了典范形制。此图绘墨兰两丛，生于草地上。兰花盛开，如彩蝶翩翩起舞。兰叶柔美舒放，清雅俊爽。全图用笔劲利，笔意绵绵，气脉不断，是赵氏画兰的代表作。

TUNE: TELLNG INNERMOST FEELING

PARTING AT RIVERS ZHANG AND GONG

— Yan Ren

Your boat sets sail after a farewell song; no grief on earth deeper appears. The feelingless river eastward flows along, the faster with my tears.

Though far away, you oft turn your head still to gaze on what you will. Where would your broken heart stay? Amid the riverside mume flowers, in one of the small crimson bowers.

sù zhōng qíng

诉 衷 情

zhāng gòng biē huāi
章 贡 别 怀

yān rēn
—— 严 仁

yì shēng shuǐ diào jiě lán zhōu① rén
一 声 水 调 解 兰 舟 ① ，人

jiān wú cǐ chóu wú qíng jiāng shuǐ dōng liú
间 无 此 愁 。无 情 江 水 东 流

qù yǔ wǒ lèi zhēng liú
去 ，与 我 泪 争 流 。

rén yǐ yuǎn gèng huí tōu kǔ níng
人 已 远 ，更 回 头 ，苦 凝

móu② duàn hún hé chù méi huā àn
眸 ② 。断 魂 何 处 ？梅 花 岸

qū xiǎo xiǎo hóng lóu
曲 ，小 小 红 楼 。

注 释

①水调，词牌名。传为隋炀帝开运河所作。兰舟，指木兰舟，古人用香木作舟，以供游览用。

②"人已远"三句：爱人已远去，却还是不停地回头张望，苦苦地凝眸注视。说明爱之深，无奈更深，只能彼此苦苦凝望远方爱人的背影。

Fishing Village Under Snow (partial) by Wang Shen, Northern Song, handscroll, color on silk, 44.4 x 219.7 cm, kept in the Palace Museum of Beijing. Wang was Emperor Yingzong's son-in-law, a contemporary of Guo Xi and an important painter of the Li Cheng school. This scroll is his representative work, expressing cultivated pleasures of a leisurely life characteristic of all literati paintings.

◎ 渔村小雪图卷（局部），北宋，王诜，绢本设色，44.4 × 219.7cm，北京故宫博物院藏。王诜是宋英宗的驸马，与郭熙同时，同为李成画派的重要画家，《渔村小雪图卷》为其传世的代表作。这幅水墨绢本横卷的作品，描绘了雪山疏柳，溪岸鱼艇，在树梢和芦苇上微染金粉，突出了文人士大夫的高情逸致，别有一番风味。

TUNE: SILK-WASHING STREAM

— Wu Wenying

I dreamed of the door parting me from my dear flower, the setting sun was mute and homing swallows drear. Her fair hands hooked up fragrant curtains of her bower.

The willowdown falls silently and spring sheds tear; the floating clouds cast shadows when the moon feels shy; the spring wind blows at night colder than autumn high.

huàn xī shā
浣 溪 沙

wú wén yīng
—— 吴文英

mén gé huā shēn mèng jiù yóu xī yáng
门 隔 花 深 梦 旧 游 ， 夕 阳
wú yǔ yàn guī chóu yù xiān xiāng dòng xiǎo lián
无 语 燕 归 愁 。 玉 纤 香 动 小 帘
gōu
钩 ① 。

luò xù wú shēng chūn duò lèi xíng yún
落 絮 无 声 春 堕 泪 ， 行 云
yǒu yǐng yuè hán xiū chūn fēng lín yè lěng
有 影 月 含 羞 ② 。 春 风 临 夜 冷
yú qiū
于 秋 。

注 释

① 玉纤：指手。
②"行云"句：形容情人姿色之美，语出宋玉《高唐赋》："旦为行云，暮为行雨。"

One Hundred Children at Play (partial) by Su Hanchen, Southern Song, handscroll, color on silk, 30.6 x 525.5 cm, kept in the Palace Museum of Taipei. In the painting two kids have a game of *weiqi* (Chinese go) while several others are watching.

◎ 长春百子（局部），南宋，苏汉臣，绢本设色，30.6 × 525.5cm（卷），台北故宫博物院藏。画面描写了几个神态各异、正在下围棋或观棋的活泼可爱的儿童。

精选 宋词与宋画

TUNE: A TWIG OF MUME BLOSSOMS

MY BOAT PASSING BY
SOUTHERN RIVER

— Jiang Jie

Can boundless vernal grief be drowned in vernal wine? My boat tossed by waves high, streamers of wineshop fly. The Farewell Ferry and the Beauty's Bridge would pine: Wind blows from hour to hour; rain falls shower by shower.

When may I go home to wash my old robe outworn, to play on silver lute and burn the incense mute? Oh, time and tide will not wait for a man forlorn: With cherry red spring dies, when green banana sighs.

yì jiǎn méi
一剪梅

zhōu guò wú jiāng ①
舟 过 吴 江

jiǎng jié
—— 蒋 捷

yí piàn chūn chóu dài jiǔ jiāo jiāng shàng zhōu
一 片 春 愁 待 酒 浇 ， 江 上 舟
yáo lóu shàng lián zhāo ② qiū niáng dù yǔ tài
摇 ， 楼 上 帘 招 。 秋 娘 渡 与 泰
niáng qiáo ③ fēng yòu piāo piāo yǔ yòu xiāo xiāo
娘 桥 ， 风 又 飘 飘 ， 雨 又 潇 潇 。
hé rì guī jiā xǐ kè páo yín zì shēng
何 日 归 家 洗 客 袍 ？ 银 字 笙
tiáo ④ xīn zì xiāng shāo ⑤ liú guāng róng yì bǎ
调 ， 心 字 香 烧 。 流 光 容 易 把
rén pāo hóng le yīng táo lǜ le bā jiāo
人 抛 ， 红 了 樱 桃 ， 绿 了 芭 蕉 。

注 释

①吴江：江苏县名。在太湖东岸，吴淞江北流经此。

②帘招：酒店的青帘迎风招展。

③秋娘渡、泰娘桥：地名，在吴江兰湾附近。

④银字笙调：镶嵌着银字的笙。调：吹弄。

⑤心字香烧：一种盘屈如"心"字的名香。杨慎《词品》："所谓心字香者，以香末萦篆成心字也。"

Silk Tree, author unknown, Southern Song, round fan, ink and wash on silk, 23.9 x 25.4 cm, kept in Shanghai Museum. The imperial-court decorative painting of the Southern Song is not as thriving as that of the Northern Song. Gigantic-sized pictures were seldom made, most on single pamphlets or round silk fans. Meanwhile, painters at this time turned to a delicate and elegant taste. In this picture the artist outlined leaves and veins with fine lines. The plant in quiet colors makes viewers feel relaxed and happy.

◎ 夜合花图，佚名，团扇，绢本水墨，23.9 × 25.4cm，上海博物馆藏。南宋的院体画相对来讲不如北宋那么繁盛，题材缩小了，大幅的巨制也不多见，多为独幅册页和纨扇画，画风也呈现出清疏淡雅的韵致。此图作者不详，为典型的南宋院体画，描绘夜合花一枝。画面细枝丰叶，花朵丛生。枝叶、花朵俱用双钩填色，叶脉勾描分明。花有含苞、将开、绽放等姿态。白花绿叶，色泽素净，耐人观赏。

TUNE: MORNING HORN AND FROSTY SKY

— Jiang Jie

A shadow's seen past window screen. Who comes to pluck flowers from my trees? You may pluck what flowers as you please. I do not know to whom they'll go.

Those near the eaves are the best among green leaves. To reach them you'd stand on tiptoe. I tell you who pluck flowers: Don't you know you will look fair if you put them aslant your hair?

注　释

①从她：任她、听她。

②檐牙：高高翘出的屋角。

shuāng tiān xiǎo jiǎo
霜 天 晓 角

jiǎng jié
—— 蒋 捷

rén yǐng chuāng shā　　　shì shuí lái zhāi
人 影 窗 纱 ， 是 谁 来 摘

huā ? zhé zé cóng tā zhé qù ①　zhī zhé
花 ？ 折 则 从 她 折 去 ① ， 知 折

qù xiàng shuí jiā
去 向 谁 家 ？

yán yá zhī zuì jiā ②　zhé shí gāo
檐 牙 枝 最 佳 ② 。 折 时 高

zhé xiē　shuō yǔ zhé huā rén dào　xū chā
折 些 。 说 与 折 花 人 道 ： 须 插

xiàng bìn biān xié
向 鬓 边 斜 。

184

Summer Mist Along the Lakeshore (partial) by Zhao Lingrang, Northern Song, handscroll, ink on silk, 19.1 x 161.3 cm, kept in Boston Museum of Fine Arts, U.S.A. Zhao was a member of the royal family living in the later stage of the Northern Song Dynasty. In this scroll the painter depicted in a fresh, chaste style a village lying at the foggy lakeside on a summer morning.

◎ 湖庄清夏图卷（局部），北宋，赵令穰，绢本墨笔，美国波士顿美术馆藏。赵令穰为宋宗室皇族，生活于北宋后期。因为出身皇族，按制不能远游，所见风光仅限于汴京、洛阳一带，所以多画京城外坡坂汀渚之景。此幅《湖庄清夏图》，描绘了湖林烟云，清丽自然，令人观之有江湖之思。或许，这是赵令穰用来抒发富贵之烦恼的一种方式吧。

TUNE: SONG OF FOUR WORDS

—Zhang Yan

Orioles sing amid leafy trees green; the breeze blows cloud-like willow down over the screen. The east wind won't be blamed by blooms; it tries to bring their flying petals to overtake spring.

My neighbor's daughter greets me with a smile and says: We should make merry when fine are the days. Where can I find her tomorrow, at which hour? In willows' shade before her bower.

sì zì lìng
四字令

—— 张炎

莺吟翠屏①，帘吹絮云。东
风也怕花嗔②，带飞花赶春。
邻娃笑迎③，嬉游趁晴。明
朝何处相寻？那人家柳阴。

注　释

①翠屏：翠绿色的屏风。

②嗔：嗔怪，责怪。

③邻娃：邻居家的小孩儿。

Landscape of Four Seasons (partial) by Liu Songnian, Southern Song, handscroll, color on silk, 41.3 x 67.9-69.5 cm each, kept in the Palace Museum of Taipei. Taking Li Tang as his model, Liu depicted in his landscape paintings the beautiful scenery of south China, and developed his own style. He divided this long scroll into four parts to separately portray the view of spring, summer, autumn and winter. It can be rated as a consummate landscape painting.

◎ 四景山水图卷（局部），南宋，刘松年，绢本设色，各41.3 × 67.9-69.5cm，台北故宫博物院藏。刘松年的山水画，虽取法于李唐，但他描写的多是江南一带的风光，又能博采众长，在艺术风格上与李唐拉开了距离，形成了自己在强劲中显出清丽细润、工整不苟的独特风格。这幅《四景山水》的笔意、皴法都有取法李唐的地方，以分成四段的长卷形式，描写了春夏秋冬四季景色，画面峭拔壮丽，工而不板，确是一幅山水佳品。

图书在版编目（ＣＩＰ）数据

精选宋词与宋画／五洲传播出版社编；许渊冲译词.
—北京：五洲传播出版社，　2005.10
ISBN 7-5085-0848-3

Ⅰ.精...　　Ⅱ.①五...②许...　　Ⅲ.①宋词－文学
欣赏－汉、英②中国画－鉴赏－中国－宋代－汉、英
Ⅳ.① I207.23 ② J212.05

中国版本图书馆 CIP 数据核字（2005）第 116861 号

宋词翻译：许渊冲
辅文翻译：邵　达
图片编辑：刘永胜

精选宋词与宋画

出版发行：五洲传播出版社

策划编辑：荆孝敏　　　　　　　责任编辑：王　莉／荆孝敏
装帧设计：缪　惟／潘宏伟／张　勇

社址：北京市海淀区北小马厂6号　　邮政编码：100038
发行电话：010-58891281　　　　　传真：010-58891281
网址：www.cicc.org.cn

制版单位：北京锦绣圣艺文化发展有限公司
印刷：北京华联印刷有限公司

开本：787×1092　1/16　印张：12.25

2005年10月第1版　2006年7月第2次印刷
ISBN 7-5085-0848-3/J·303　　　　　定价：78.00元